The Gentle Art of Swedish Death Cleaning

Isabella V. Allen

Swedish Life Organization Benefits from Death Cleaning

It can be difficult to find time to stay organized in a world where we are all so busy and feel like there isn't enough time in the day. Not your typical let's-clean-up-this-messy-house organization, but a holistic approach to keeping track of your belongings and life at home. Swedish Death Cleaning is more of a lifestyle than a decluttering trend, with significant benefits for both your home and your peace of mind. Here are some of the advantages of using this unique decluttering method for death cleaning.

Death cleaning, or Döstädning in Swedish, was popularized by author Margareta Magnusson and describes a series of decluttering and tidying aimed at easing the burden on your loved ones after your death. In essence, it is a method of gradually downsizing your household in the second half of your life. The idea is that if you do this, your loved ones won't have to deal with your belongings after you're gone.

However, getting rid of unnecessary items as you get older has personal benefits as well. As you get older, you won't have to deal with the stress of having a lot of clutter in your house, which makes cleaning easier. If you get rid of things you don't need right now, you won't have to deal with them later in life. This could include getting rid of clothes you don't wear anymore, books you don't intend to read again, or knickknack that just collects dust.

There are several advantages to death cleaning, and unlike other decluttering methods, they are long-lasting. This is primarily due to the fact that Swedish Death Cleaning is a very slow process. That is, you gradually develop new habits and acclimate to less clutter over time, in tandem with your downsizing efforts.

Stress Management

One of the most obvious Swedish death cleaning benefits is that it reduces the stress associated with having too much clutter in your home. When you have a lot of stuff around you, you may feel overwhelmed, even subconsciously, making it difficult to relax. Cleaning can be difficult when you have a lot of belongings. Slowly reducing your household inventory is liberating in that you have less to maintain and care for. There is less to be concerned about.

Organization for a Better Life

You're less likely to lose track of things if you have a place for everything. This also means that you will be less distracted by the clutter around you. And that means more time to do the things you enjoy, the things that are more important to you than dusting and organizing. Indeed, death cleaning can help you live a more fulfilling life in your later years. You'll have less to deal with later in life if you start now.

Asserting Your Last Will and Testament Through Death Cleaning

When you begin your Swedish death cleaning journey, it is common to begin reserving specific items for family members. Maybe your nephew is interested in your vintage mid-century shelving unit, or maybe your best friend's daughter has always admired your well-organized luxury handbag collection. These are items you intend to keep, but you can start making a list of who gets what later. If you aren't ready to write an actual testament, doing this in a household inventory spreadsheet is a great place to start.

You can tell your people which items you want to donate and which should be discarded so they know what to do with your belongings.

You are free to keep your sentimental items

Some may be concerned that if they begin decluttering with the Swedish death cleaning method and get rid of everything they don't love or use, they will have to declutter all of their sentimental items as well. Not so! You can keep the things that are truly special to you and matter the most when you are death cleaning.

Designating a special box or bin like this for old love letters, clippings, or other nostalgic items allows you to access them whenever you want without them getting in the way. Plus, culling your sentimental items to fit in this box shows that you truly value what you're keeping. This leads me to one of our next death cleaning advantages:

You keep what you want and use what you have

When you're in the process of death cleaning and wondering if you should get rid of something, think about whether you love and use it, just like you would with any other decluttering method. If you don't, it probably shouldn't be taking up space in your house.

If you like something but don't use it, consider donating it or passing it on to a friend or neighbor. You may discover that you adore something but simply do not have the space for it. Or that you don't use something you adore because you're afraid of ruining it or don't know how to care for it.

Swedish death cleaning allows you to consider such possessions and examine your own behavior. Personally, I think you should wear your Chanel jacket to the supermarket, eat from your inherited fine bone china, and drink the vintage wine you've been saving in the cellar. Life is short, and if you're attached to certain possessions, don't be afraid to enjoy them in your daily life.

The Transition to Downsizing is Made Easier by Death Cleaning

One of the most significant advantages of death cleaning is that it gradually eases your household into downsizing. If you know you'll be moving into a smaller home or apartment in the near future, Swedish death cleaning is the decluttering method for you.

The best way to begin is to gradually declutter the shed, attic, basement, garage, and larger items such as furniture. You've already won half the battle by the time you get to the smaller items like books and clothing. When the time comes to look for a smaller home or consider moving into a flat where you won't have to worry about yard or roof maintenance, your household inventory will already be much more manageable, and you'll have a better idea of how small you can downsize.

Death cleaning is a fantastic concept to keep in mind as you approach middle age and begin to consider the next stage of your life. It's an excellent way to gradually begin decluttering your home, organizing your belongings, preparing for downsizing, or simply making life easier for yourself—and your family and friends later on. You'll reap a variety of death cleaning benefits by starting in your forties, so you'll have far less stress dealing with excess clutter in your home when you're old.

Contents

Chapter 1: What is Decluttering

***

What is clutter? Clutter may be defined as anything, like a heap of mess that needs to be sorted out because it has gone way out of control.

Clutter is mostly caused by postponed decision making. Meaning that overthinking where to put certain things, or even whether to throw them away or not can cause serious clutter in your home.

When you have a lot of things in your house that you don't want or need, things that take up unnecessary space and cause discomfort, it is advised that you declutter.

Now, let's discuss decluttering. Decluttering is a cleaning technique that involves the removal of certain things in a particular space or area that you no longer have a use for, in order that the space looks better, cleaner and is more useful. It may also be seen as a way of organizing different things in a place by getting rid of the not so useful things.

Decluttering your space is one of the best things you can do in your home. It helps keep that space more organized, and it also makes that space or area more accessible.

An organized area or workspace does not just look good; it also enhances productivity and can open your mind to new ideas. It improves you psychologically in ways you would never believe existed.

Benefits of Decluttering

There are various benefits of decluttering your space, but some of the most important ones are have been selected out of the multitude, and they include:

Better First Impressions

When a person walks into your house and comes to the conclusion that he or she would be more comfortable in a junkyard, that person would likely not come over again. A tidy and uncluttered space or area says a lot about who a person is. It might just send the wrong signal to anyone seeing it, that you are untidy, and, in many cases, you are not. Even at work, when you have a cluttered workspace, you tend to push away customers or clients. That could even paint a poor picture of you to your bosses. Just imagine your boss walking up to your desk and wondering about the reasons why you were hired. But with a decluttered space, you will not only make the best first impressions but also maintain a good and healthy relationship with your boss, your friends, and your family.

Improved Comfort

When a space is cluttered, it feels like that place has room for anything. How would you be in your house and feel like your things are closing in on you? It's like a scene from a very horrifying movie. There's no actual space to do anything; you can barely walk around or take more rest. And come to think of it, how can you rest when you are not comfortable? If you are not comfortable in your own home, it should not be referred to as home anymore. This is what clutter can do in a home. But when you have a decluttered home, you will seem more at ease, and you will rest better.

Even at work. How can you work when there is no actual space for work? When you feel like the space on your desk is shrinking more and more by the day. Look if you keep a file on your desk today, and vigorously look for it the next day amongst the other files on the desk, it means you seriously need to declutter. When you have a tidy workspace, it gives room for more development and growth. It improves your thinking and also revitalizes your mind.

Improved Confidence

Who doesn't love being confident? Everybody does. When you have a decluttered space, you will feel comfortable to let anyone into your house or room as the case may be.

You cannot be living in a madhouse and feel confident letting someone in. It would even reduce your confidence more than you think. Many people would say nothing when they are with you but wait until they go outside, it would go so viral that the Daily Show would pick up the news.

But when you have a tidy home or room, you will feel so confident to let anyone in, no matter how impromptu the visit may be.

This also applies to your workplace. When you constantly have to look for something on your work desk, especially when your boss urgently needs it, it makes you less confident around them. Let's imagine your manager sending you to get a file you have been working on for a while, and you spend close to three hours trying to get it, when we all know that you don't need a three-hour flight to get to your office and back.

What impression of yourself are you setting for your boss?

But when you have an organized workspace, finding files and documents would take less than a minute, which means that you will be doing your job better, faster, and more effectively and with a whole lot of confidence.

Better Health

This is probably one of the most, if not the most, important benefit of having a decluttered space. You should know that clutter comes with a lot of germs and disease-carrying organisms which would cripple your immune system in a way that a harmless cough could send you to the emergency room. Yes, just like that, you could be the reason for your predicament. If you live in a cluttered space and you are experiencing symptoms of illness, it's not from people outside; nope, it's from your mess.

Even at work, a desk is a place where these organisms can thrive and multiply, especially when it is not being cleaned regularly and especially when they have a lot of places to hide. You could be going home sick from work because of your own work area, which means that you are the reason. This may not only affect you, but it could also affect a lot of other people who come in contact with you or the germ-infested space you call a desk.

Improved Time Management

With much less items to be concerned with in your house, it is only consequential that you would spend less time having to clean and arrange things or look for them. This is because you have made a place for the few things you decided to keep and, if you can sustain the decluttering, you may not have to spend so much time cleaning out your house again.

The Importance of a Decluttering Work Plan

The importance of a decluttering work plan is multifaceted, but the main importance is that it helps you clean up places in order of priority. It helps you to make progress any time you clean up or declutter. The main aim of having a decluttering work plan is to enable you to make more progress in decluttering, and if you are not making much progress, it helps you see where you got it wrong, so that you can easily pick up from where you left off.

If you don't have a very effective work plan, you will just end up spinning your wheels, and after the first and second day you might just give up. Because clutter sometimes is overwhelming, you feel like you are not making any progress, but when you have a proper work plan you will know that you are making subsequent progress in decluttering.

You can make this plan based on how free you are during the week or the month. You should also know that if you overexert yourself by not giving yourself breaks during the work plan, you will give up as fast as you started.

It should be like a work timetable, where you have breaks in between work hours. Why exactly do you think those breaks exist on your work timetable? It's for you to relax, recharge and to let your creative juices flow.

When creating your work plan, the pen is literally in your hands; you can make it in any way that suits you. You can make it a one-week plan, a one-month plan, a two-month plan, or more. Some people even have declutter work plans that go as long as one year. Yes, a year! You can imagine how much clutter that could resolve.

Your work plan should be spacious and not cluttered like your mess. It should be flexible and malleable.

This work plan has proven to be extremely useful. You should know that if you have other areas in your house that have clutter which was not mentioned in the work plan, you could treat them the same way. Also, you should try and give yourself several breaks during the whole workload if not, it will take a toll on you.

Time Management

Time management can be described as the ability to manage one's time so that they complete tasks effectively.

Time management is one of the main limitations of decluttering. When you are not able to manage your time in every aspect of your life, how can you declutter your home? The decluttering work plan above can only work when you have proper time management.

At this point, all you have to do is to sit down and create a timetable for everything that you do. It would help you manage your time better and be more effective. But if you possess good time management qualities, you are one step closer to decluttering your home.

Clutter is one of the main reasons why people feel insecure about themselves and their space. If you don't manage it now, it could affect you in the future, because by now we all know that clutter does not just magically disappear. It takes time, effort, and a whole lot of determination

Chapter 2: Swedish Death Cleaning

***

While the topic might seem rather dark, it really is a harmless one — a helpful one, to be precise. So, rest assured, we won't be discussing anything related to giving cadavers a sound bath or whipping them into shape for an afterlife in a lab. And neither would we be discussing about hiding bodies and cleaning up a bloody room after a John Wick scene.

Moreover, if the little rhetoric above doesn't serve to allay your fears either because the topic has Scandinavian written all over it, then perhaps it's time we introduced you to the subject and explore it from its very roots.

The Origin of Swedish Death Cleaning

Every hero in comics and movies always has an origin story — one which tells of their development through different phases until they became the heroes as we know them, and what prompted them into donning signature costumes and taking on responsibilities.

Consider Swedish Death Cleaning as a hero, and this, it's origin story.

Swedish Death Cleaning derives its name from a word in the Swedish vocabulary, döstädning. This word is roughly a complex formation of two other words, namely "do" and "stadning". The former implies "death" and the latter means "cleaning." Thus, a literal translation of the word in English gives rise to the phrase, "death cleaning".

If you're still wondering about its Scandinavian roots, here's how it came to be. Firstly, keep in mind that Swedish Death Cleaning isn't a fancy way in which the Swedes clean up their dead. No. On the contrary, the concept of Swedish Death Cleaning was simply popularized by the Swedish artist, Margareta Magnusson who authored the book, The Gentle Art of Swedish Death Cleaning — How to Make Your Loved Ones' Lives Easier and Your Own Life More Pleasant (2017).

Magnusson, who describes herself as one between the ages of 80 and 100 years, has had to practice the art of Swedish Death Cleaning quite a few times. She has survived her friends, parents, husband, and in-laws; for whom she was involved in cleaning out their houses. From this point, it can be deduced that Magnusson has had quite an experience in going through the death cleaning process over and over again with different persons. This connotes different memories, levels of clutter, and a sense of hoarding. However, the intriguing part of Magnusson's work is the essence of emotions she put into the process. This singular factor is what sparked a trend of the Swedish Death Cleaning and earned her some fame.

How Does Swedish Death Cleaning Work?

Having discussed the origin of the subject, let's consider how it works.

Let's begin by considering the term death in the name. The word doesn't necessarily imply that someone has to have died for the process of death cleaning to be executed. On the contrary, it is more indicative of the mortality of our lives — a subject we seldom ever want to talk about or spend a fraction of a second thinking about. However, it's imperative we understand that our willful ignorance on the subject of our own death doesn't quell its inevitability. Eventually, we are all going to die; you, I, everyone. But just because we have no control over our own mortality doesn't mean that we can't take control of how we affect others when we are no more.

The general idea is to be mindful of our immortality and relate it to the stuff we obtain during our lifetime. As much as we won't be here forever, our stuff won't be either. So, rather than go about stocking up on stuff like we could manipulate the time stone and live forever, it's best we approach obtaining things in the latter ages of our life with a keen sense of minimalism and objectivity. If you must keep a thing, it has to be something you would absolutely use, not a thing you feel sentimental attachments to.

On the other hand, cleaning as mentioned in the subject is not suggestive of traditional cleaning with brooms and dustpans or mops. Rather, the cleaning mentioned refers to the process of decluttering your home and your life. You would be surprised how much clutter takes up valuable space in your home and your life. In the event that you can't imagine yourself owning any clutter, let's see the meaning of the word. Clutter refers to any array of things in a chaotic or jumbled up state. Ring any bells yet? Perhaps not. Let me elaborate further.

Do you have that stash of stuff which comprises basically everything and anything? What's more, do you seldom ever go through the stash or do away with any of it? So, it's just there gathering dust and muck; neither adding to your life but taking up valuable space. But why is it you can't just take down the stash? Sometimes the stash is made up of stuff which we have associated with the memories of people we hold dear. And even when these things are literally of no use to us, we consider them too valuable and just can't bring ourselves to do away with them. That's why the broken fishing rod still lies in the basement, because it reminds you of your fishing days with a good friend you lost to cancer. That's also why you still haven't let go of that set of china from your dearly departed mother, even though it is chipped at the rims and you have many others you do use.

Piecing together the words, we can deduce a definition for Swedish Death Cleaning as a step-by-step process of ridding your home of clutter in a bid to prepare for your departure (eventual death). Although this meaning could sound outrightly grim, it is a rather healthy and practical approach born of an emotional concern for the persons who would survive you and would be left with the job of dealing with the stuff you leave behind. Hence, Swedish Death Cleaning is more like evaluating your life and the things you keep. You begin by evaluating the influence of the particular thing in your life; does it inspire feelings of happiness in you, and would it be useful in the short or long run? Having evaluated the thing from your standpoint, the next thing is to evaluate its effect on the lives of the people to whom it would fall after your departure. Would it bring them as much joy as it brought you, or would it just be another piece of clutter that'll make them cringe?

But why in the first place do we gather up stuff year in year out? Magnusson was of the opinion that all our clutter can be traced to three major sources. However, of all three of them, the one most accountable for our behavior is instincts. Our natural tendency to hunt for stuff and gather the ones we find pleasing is an innate quality acquired from our primate ancestors who lived and thrived by hunting, gathering and hoarding. It is quite logical now why we apply this innate quality to our lifestyles (Magnusson, 2017).

In this day and age, we justify our attitude of gathering and hoarding stuff by the thought that they would one day be handed down to loved ones. And while there is no vanity in such thoughts, and they are indeed very good ones, we forget something important. The times are changing, and with the changing time comes the evolution of taste and fashion. As such, the very things you found tasteful, the ones which brought you joy may not appear so to the person(s) who will clean out your stuff when you are gone. It would neither bring them joy nor be found tasteful by them. It would just be another piece in a pile of clutter.

While this could be a rather tough truth to take in, that's the way things would pan out. This doesn't imply that they don't want to remember you or want you out of their lives for good. No, it's just the natural order of things. You have your stuff as they have theirs, and there are a lot of other ways to remember you other than by your hand-me-downs. I mean, hoarding loads of clutter is one way they would not forget you in a long time. But not in a good way. If the people who go through your stuff and clean out your home after your demise have to spend valuable time, energy and money on mindless clutter, it is safe to say they will remember you and that experience as long as they live.

And believe you me, you do not want to be known as the relative, parent or friend who made others use up valuable resources in getting rid of clutter. Sure, you made nice cookies and were fun to hang out with while you lived, but they'll remember they paid a fortune to dispose of the stash of worthless cookie jars you shoved into the attic, and all your broken and dysfunctional fishing equipment stored in the basement. How very nice of you!

The Swedish Death Cleaning Method is more of an emotional and thorough process than it is given credit for. It is all about laying aside the sentimental baggage which only serves to bring clutter into your life and home. By evaluating your lifestyle and regulating what you keep or discard, you will be making it easier for yourself and others. By so doing, you leave them with an imperishable part of you that they will cherish for the rest of their lives — memories rather than clutter. And although it might seem like Swedish Death Cleaning is only beneficial to the people surviving you, it also holds some benefit for you on a personal level. Studies in the fields of sociology and psychology have revealed that the process of going through your own stuff, cutting down on clutter and doing a routine cleanup is quite helpful (Boyes, 2018). Not only would you be able to evaluate your reasons for keeping some stuff, you would also be able to relive some memories from memorabilia as well as keep your life and home in order. As such, it is advisable you begin practicing the Swedish Death Cleaning Method to enjoy your life and influence after you are gone.

The Effects of Swedish Death Cleaning and How It Can Change Your Life

The Swedish Death Cleaning Method has several life changing effects on the lives of those who practice it. Some are listed below:

1. It helps you understand and cope with the actuality that death is inevitable

However grim we consider the discussion of death to be, it is something we have to talk about eventually. But if you are still unable to stomach it, the subject of death cleaning is another way to approach the topic. The art of disposing of stuff you no longer consider valuable teaches a valuable lesson that sooner or later, everything expires. This includes us as people. The reality of an expiration (death) is something we'll have to come to terms with eventually.

Swedish Death Cleaning involves going through your stuff and deciding on what to keep or do away with. In this process, you get the chance to go through your own history. You get a reminder of how far you have come, who you were and who you have now grown into. It redefines how you see yourself, which in turn would prompt how you want others to see you when you are no more. Consider the Swedish Death Cleaning as a build-up to your legacy.

Also, you will need to consider that someone will have to deal with all you have gathered and hoarded either during your life or after it. Here, you are prompted to make the call of who it would be: you or the ones who survive you.

It's no hidden fact that there is an age you attain when you become incapable of doing all the stuff you used to do when you were younger. You tire out easily, find it difficult to be up all day with little to no rest, etcetera. Even at this moment before your passing, you still face the challenge of knowing you are not as fit as you used to be. Let's not even talk about the increasing tendency of having a disability of some sort at this period. In practicing Swedish Death Cleaning, you literally prepare yourself to accept the changes going on within and around you. You submit to the reality that you are passing but not in a bad way, and you accept it. You don't feel sad or sorry for yourself because the routine prepares you mentally and emotionally.

Further research on the subject reveals that Swedish Death Cleaning is best carried out sooner rather than later, when you are still able to do things on your own. The reason being that you become less likely to clean out your own stuff and trim them down as you grow older. The whole process of cleaning gets more laborious as you age owing to the emotional, physical, and cognitive effort which goes into the process.

2. It improves your chances of happiness

The Swedish Death Cleaning Method can also be interpreted as a practical approach to minimalism because it fulfills all the benefits the latter offers. It is why people get attracted to it the same way certain people are attracted to smaller houses and mobile homes and opt for them in lieu of regular size, stationary, traditional houses. But how does this in any way affect your overall level of happiness? Good question. You needn't win the lottery or happen on a slab of uncut diamond to be happy. Although it would be rather funny to deny the joy either could bring into one's life, however, the key to happiness lies in focusing on what makes you happy, not the things you perceive could bring happiness. It is why a popular maxim suggests that happiness cannot be purchased. Even though, sometimes, what brings us happiness actually can.

Anyway, the point is, cleaning out your stuff and cutting down on clutter will help tune your focus to the important part(s) of your life you couldn't possibly have seen through the whole pile of rubble. Parts that have been concealed beneath tons of dirt, and other needless stuff you struggle to gather and hoard. In psychology, minimalistic behavior stems from the concept of happiness being a function of experiences, memories, and relationships rather than memorabilia and stuff (Nowak, 2004). That is, the minimalistic approach of cherishing good memories, great relationships and wonderful experiences supersedes the satisfaction obtained from tangible stuff kept in memory of things, places or people. The same applies to the aim of Swedish Death Cleaning. Instead of spending your lifetime hunting and gathering things you consider good enough to pass down to others, you let go of accumulating material wealth and resort to making yourself a source of happiness to be remembered now that you still live, and when you will be gone.

But to do this, you have to declutter your life and home by disposing of all the material items which blind and inhibit you. Only when this is done will you be able to perceive and reach for the things that are truly important — the tangible sources of happiness that don't wither with age and can be spread to others. In this regard, studies have proved that if you put your time and effort into securing material wealth in stuff and riches, you stand a much higher chance of not finding happiness, as well as ending up with poor relationships and intimacy, anxiety and a poor sense of self-worth. It sounds completely logical why this is the case with materialistic pursuits.

In our world today, there are tons of opportunities to get new stuff, what with the endless manufacturing of diverse products which promise to bring certain levels of happiness into our lives. While this can sound quite thrilling, it is no doubt an overwhelming indulgence. It is for this reason the concept of cutting down on the clutter taking up space in your life is upheld. Because it pushes against the overwhelming clutter in the world we live in and helps us find true happiness.

3. It cuts down on stress and overload, helping you achieve more

A final upside of embracing Swedish Death Cleaning is its impact on your mind and body. The whole system of the Swedish Death Cleaning is quite therapeutic; it reduces your level of stress and prevents you from getting overwhelmed. How does this work? Easy peasy. The mind has some sort of silly trick of fleeing by feigning tiredness and whatnot when it perceives work. As such, if your living area is stuffed up and filled with clutter, you would easily feel too overwhelmed to want to clean up. And the longer you procrastinate, the more you stress about getting the job done.

But if you take the time out to momentarily practice the Swedish Death Cleaning every day, you will go through your days living in an environment that is clean, organized and free of clutter. In the process, your stress lessens, and you become more focused on the real things that matter. Also, the fact that you have little to nothing to stress about from little chores around the home to bigger challenges gives you a sense of satisfaction that you have your life under control. Studies in psychotherapy back up this argument with a revelation that one's appearance is the result of the ongoing on their insides and vice versa. As such, you become less likely to feel any stress or anxiety whatsoever if your outer, external environment is decluttered, and in order. Several studies have gone on to prove how clutter influences stress and anxiety and lowers productivity rate (Palmer, 2017).

Tips for Following the Swedish Death Cleaning Method

Know When to Begin

Knowing the right time to begin is crucial in the Swedish Death Cleaning process. In her book, Magnusson opined that the age of 65 and above is a good time for you to begin decluttering and trimming down your properties. But Swedish Death Cleaning isn't limited to this age of individuals alone, persons of other ages can also learn from its concept of minimalism and live a clutter-free life.

Understand the Reality That No One Wants Your Stuff

This is arguably one of the harshest truths of the world today. As much as we hunt and gather up stuff which we want to pass on to others, the truth is that the craze for hand-me-downs has ended. Only a relatively small populace is interested in taking their parents stuff. The vast majority of us do not care to.

And it isn't that the second group aren't appreciative enough. No. Matter of fact, a ton of factors influence their choices. For one, there may not be a market to sell some of the stuff. Another thing is the reluctance to add more stuff to what they already own. No one would want to upset their lifestyle because of hand-me-downs. There is also the consideration of modernity and change in tastes. For instance, rather than taking bulky old furniture as a hand-me-down, some people would prefer to stick to modern, lightweight, and space-saving furniture.

Know What to Keep

Often times the clutter we keep is comprised mainly of memorabilia which we rarely ever consider doing away with. However, we have got to learn that we needn't keep physical things to maintain a memory. The mind is wired to store all your precious memories, so souvenirs and memorabilia just add to your clutter instead. Look through your stuff and take note of the souvenirs and memorabilia that you have somehow not disposed of even though they are of no use to you.

Know Where to Begin

It's not enough to want to declutter your home alone. It's also important you know from whence to begin in order for the process to be effective. Experts advise it is best you don't begin with your photographs first. The reason being that pictures evoke memories and would require quite some time to decide which ones to keep or discard. In this vein, it's advisable you begin with your closet. Begin the Swedish Death Cleaning from there by going through your clothes and pick out the items that no longer fit and the ones you don't wear anymore.

Master the Art of Gifting

Perhaps your relatives don't want your stuff, but it doesn't mean others won't. Try gifting some of the stuff that constitutes clutter in your home to others who might be in need of them. And by clutter, the implied meaning is useful things that you don't use, not stuff that is useless in itself. As such, when you are headed out for your next meet-and-greet or a family dinner, don't hesitate to pack a gift for someone out of the things you don't use. As much as this helps cut down on clutter, you also get to make a good impression.

Document the Important Stuff

One vital aspect of Swedish Death Cleaning is indulging other people in the process. It is a healthy practice for many different reasons. For instance, it would improve your accountability. Since others are involved now, there would be people to inform and help you when you slack off. Also, you can seize the moment to declare to your family and friends what you would want them to do after your demise. It is at this point you should begin documenting any important records associated with you such as login information, passwords, credit and debit cards, wills, properties, and other vital knowledge they would otherwise be unaware of when you pass on. From this point on, make it a priority to properly store your remaining possessions and keep only the things you truly need.

Ensure It Lasts Longer

It's never easy beginning a new practice. As a matter of fact, studies reveal that it takes the average person at least two months to adopt a habit. In this vein, to ensure the habit of Swedish Death Cleaning abides with you, consider rewarding yourself every now and then as you make the effort to downsize. You can do this in diverse ways. Try seeing a movie, going on a date with your friends, or doing something you have always wanted to do like knitting, skiing, bowling, etc. Just keep yourself from replacing everything you downsized with newer items.

Size Matters

In Swedish Death Cleaning, size is everything. Thus, instead of beginning with smaller items like mail, photos, books and personal papers, start with the large items which take up much space and work your way to the smaller ones.

Sell or Donate Your Stuff

If after gifting some of your stuff you still have quite a lot left that you would like to do away with, consider donating them or selling them for money. You can make a donation to a charitable cause or organize a yard sale. If before your demise you don't practice Swedish Death Cleaning and organize your stuff, chances are things you considered important or gift-worthy would be sold at auctions or disposed of altogether.

Frequently Declutter Your Home

Decluttering your home regularly will help you maintain a hold on your possessions. Consider your stuff to be a haircut, if you visit the salon regularly you will be able to keep your hair trimmed and avoid overgrown hair. Keep in mind to put on an apron or work with a bag as you declutter, in case you have to collect stuff which was wrongly placed.

How Does Swedish Death Cleaning Differ from Other Traditional Methods of Cleaning?

If Swedish Death Cleaning is just another type of cleaning among many others - like KonMari and Feng Shui - what then is all the fuss about, right? I mean, sure the name has somewhat of a grim ring to it which should pique anyone's curiosity, but is it really worth the hype? Well, let's find out by juxtaposing it to other cleaning methods known today.

Practicing Swedish Death Cleaning Involves Making Important Decisions

Unlike traditional cleaning and other popular decluttering approaches that have gained fame in recent times like the Feng Shui and KonMari, Swedish Death Cleaning involves more than just mops and brooms. Matter of fact, making the effort to practice Swedish Death Cleaning is an important decision in itself.

It spans way beyond going through your stuff for things you don't use, cutting down on clutter and organizing your living or workspace. Unlike in other cleaning methods where the aim is to clean up to improve your health and standard of living, the purpose for Swedish Death Cleaning is to better your life, however long is left of it, as well as to make things easier on the people you leave behind. No other cleaning method aside from Swedish Death Cleaning makes any allowances for considering crucial decisions pertaining to your dying wishes, will, entitlements, etcetera.

Although it might seem as though the Swedish Death Cleaning

Method is especially focused on death, that is not the case. Instead, it can be perceived to be an all-rounder which everyone needs to practice in the latter stages of their lives, if not throughout all of it. The decision-making aspect of Swedish Death Cleaning is all about trimming down the clutter in your life as you age to make things easier for you and your survivors in and towards the final moments of your life.

The Concept Behind Swedish Death Cleaning Has No Age Limit

Isn't Swedish Death Cleaning targeted at the old and dying lot? Not quite. Although it focuses expressly on the aging to help give them a much easier life at the later stages, the conceptual framework behind the Swedish Death Cleaning Method is in itself not limited to a specific age alone. What makes up the conceptual framework, you might wonder? There are two major factors, namely minimalism and decluttering.

Both factors aren't age specific, as such, anyone who is willing can employ them in leading their lives. Even though in her book, Margareta Magnusson was of the opinion that Swedish Death Cleaning is particularly beneficial for persons aged 50 years and above, anyone can in fact practice it. When compared to other traditional cleaning methods in this regard, it's easy to deduce that little to no thought at all is given to the age factor. I mean, who considers age when it's all dusting and mopping and organizing and maximizing space? Absolutely no one. But Swedish Death Cleaning is quite sensitive to the age factor. This is why it is practiced differently across ages — because it offers concepts for anyone willing to cut down on clutter, arrange their space and make their life easier.

It Focuses on the Before and After Stages of a Person's Life

Other cleaning methods focus more on the surroundings, how to tidy up and make it better, not the individual(s) involved in the process, their preparedness or death. For this reason, the Swedish Death Cleaning stands out because cognizance is not given to the immediate environment alone and the effects of tidying up within a relatively short period. More precisely, Swedish Death Cleaning focuses on how constant, regular cleaning can affect one within the period of living and after one is dead.

Thus, unlike regular traditional cleaning, it is effective both during the life of a person and afterwards. For instance, other traditional methods of cleaning would only serve to keep the house tidy and organized, even KonMari which is held in high regard goes only as far as clearing out just the things that no longer bring you joy or are of use to you. Swedish Death Cleaning on the other hand rids your life and space of stuff that would neither yield joy for others nor be used by them after your passing. In this vein, other cleaning methods would still require your stuff to be checked and downsized — a process which can be both tiring and expensive. In the case of Swedish Death Cleaning, you needn't have to worry about your things being messed up when you're gone. The reason being that you were prepared for your demise and have taken the time to put your property in order.

Timing

Other cleaning methods can be done and over with within a few hours of a day. The Swedish Death Cleaning method, however, can't. It is simply too much of a process to be wrapped up within a couple of minutes. Consider it to be a process of evaluating your life, history and belongings from over the years. It simply cannot be completed in a day. And it's not because it's more complex than other methods of cleaning. No. It's that a lot goes into the process ranging from precise decision-making to in-depth analysis to adequate preparation and documentation, among other things. For this reason, it has to be carried out gradually in a logical manner. Thus, it could take many weeks to finish, or the entirety of one's life.

Also, since it is aimed at changing one's life for the better, it cannot be rushed. This is sometimes the exact opposite of regular cleaning methods which can be hurried for faster results.

In conclusion, while Swedish Death Cleaning encompasses a lot of concepts which serve to help you create an enjoyable life free of clutter in a healthy space for yourself and the people succeeding you, other cleaning methods promise little to nothing different from tidiness — a factor which can become compromised with passing time.

Chapter 3: The KonMari Method

***

Named after the acclaimed cleaning consultant, Netflix show host, and bestselling author who came up with the method, Marie Kondo, the KonMari decluttering technique focuses on the emotions tied to an item rather than the space it occupies or how long it has been with the owner. If it inspires positivity and joy, then it stays. Otherwise, you must make the decision to let it go. Another unique characteristic of KonMari is that the decluttering is not done from one room to the next.

Instead, items are segregated into five categories. The first is clothes. Empty your wardrobe and determine those ones that hold no particular value anymore. For instance, you may have outgrown some of them or your style could have changed. Once you have done this, you may return those few clothes that you are certain to continue wearing.

Next, are books. You know those paperbacks from a time you can no longer remember? Maybe you should consider donating some of them. If you're really attached to the content in the book, maybe give e-books a try. Books with worn out covers and pages may also be discarded. Following right after are those precious papers you can't seem to part with. Drafts, to-dos, now-irrelevant documents, and others that fill your waste bin and litter different parts of your house should be done away with. Thinking about it, you may conclude that there wouldn't be much to dispose of in the paper category. After searching though, you just might find much more than you had imagined.

Komono, which is Japanese for small things or young person, may also be translated to mean miscellaneous. This is another category in the KonMari method. To continue with this decluttering method at this stage, you are to get rid of all things that do not fit into the three categories above, hold no value, and to which you are not emotionally attached. This may account for the largest pile. We all have Komonos and, as such, would not have difficulty to identify and be rid of them.

Finally, you can concentrate on sorting out items that you are emotionally invested in. While such things may be the hardest to throw away (it may seem like a piece of your heart will leave with the item), it is not impossible to decide and act accordingly. To make it easier, you may gift such items to those you care. When using the KonMari style of decluttering, sentimental involvement with certain items is not enough reason for them to stay. But there is one emotion which, according to Marie Kondo, is a determining factor for any particular item to remain with you: joy.

If it brings joy to your heart when you look at or use it, then you should keep it. In using KonMari, you strip your life down to only those things that inspire feelings of bliss, happiness, and love. By so doing, you would find yourself to be more productive, positive, and less moody.

Visualization is a key part of the KonMari technique. Being able to see what your house, office, and other areas should be like and what certain spaces could be used for is essential to moving forward with KonMari. Consider each room and conjure images of what the perfect uncluttered lifestyle would be. It's also an important factor in continuing to use this organization method.

One necessary quality for anyone trying out the KonMari method is commitment. Using this technique, an individual may be done with cleaning in little more than a couple of hours. But this depends on how much clutter is being organized and how quickly the person can come to a decision about what stays and goes. Some may take as many as three months to satisfactorily declutter their homes. Another reason for commitment is that the individual must have completed one category before moving to the next. For example, if someone using KonMari is not done organizing their books, they should not skip to arranging their sentimental items. In abiding by the rules of KonMari, they must also not flit from room to room but organize each category in a particular room before moving on.

Hard as it might be for someone who is not used to a minimalist lifestyle to wrap their heads around KonMari, the reward is usually quite an incentive; your dream life where every item, in the words of Marie Kondo, 'sparks joy' in you and your life is unburdened by clutter.

A Few Things to Remember About the KonMari Method

1. Unpack and untag almost immediately after a purchase

In the philosophy of Kondo, leaving the items you purchased in their packs makes them seem like goods in a store rather than your property to be used. This increases the likelihood that they will sit unused for a long time. For example, when you have lots of clothes in your wardrobe, and you purchase another only to leave it packed and tagged. There is every chance that you will not touch it, and it won't really feel like your own until you tear the tag off, remove it from the pack, and put it on.

2. Ask yourself if the item inspires (sparks) happiness or joy when you look at or touch it, or if it is valuable

This is the central message of KonMari. The deciding factor must always be that the item makes you happy simply by looking at or touching it. But this is not to say that you should part with every item you are not sentimental about. After all, what emotions are you expected to feel about a curtain or hairbrush? In such cases, you must decide whether or not that property holds any present or future value. Is it still functional and efficient, or is there a better replacement? These questions will make it easier to decide which items should be discarded and those you should retain.

3. Make sure there is a specific place for every item

In most houses, while a few items have their permanent positions, things are usually kept in no particular place. Bags, books, remote controls, the children's toys, etc. occupy whichever is the nearest storage space to the owner. This makes for a haphazard lifestyle and may cause the individual to misplace their belongings. In an ordered environment, one can, without much thought, tell where a particular object is supposed to be and find it there. The way of order is also the KonMari way. Every object should have its permanent place and should always be returned there after use.

4. Be disciplined enough to follow the ordered manner of organization

KonMari is one decluttering technique with strict rules about the steps which must be followed. To miss or mix up the steps would mean not getting the full reward of this method of organization. Before choosing to try out KonMari, you must have made up your heart to abide by the steps and order which characterizes the technique. As a result of how long it sometimes takes to completely declutter using KonMari, some find it difficult to stick to the rules. They abandon the steps and choose to do it their own way. As such, they might not be able to maintain the tidiness brought about by the decluttering for very long.

5. The key point is not minimalism, but joy

Truly, KonMari appears like the typical minimalist approach to decluttering, where the goal is very few objects present and there is a lot of white space. But KonMari is not about the possession of few properties. It, in no way, suggests to anyone that they should throw out all or most of what they have. In fact, the philosophy behind KonMari is not centered on what one must give up or discard, but on the few things which they must keep. It is about living a life that is less cluttered and, more importantly, in which every corner of the room(s) brings joy to the individual.

6. You should give yourself a deadline

It is common human nature to procrastinate and hope to do tomorrow what could be done now. We look for a reason why today is not suitable for a particular activity and, as you probably know from experience, find many. It is for the sake of procrastination that we must give ourselves deadlines. For Marie Kondo, it should take no more than six months to completely declutter and organize using the KonMari method. But, depending on how motivated you are, the free time you have, and the size of the place you are organizing, you may decide to be a little more strict on yourself.

7. Thank the items you are about to let go of

Yes, this may seem like hocus pocus and feel more than a little corny to you, but many who have given it a try find that doing this is liberating. This is especially so when the item you are parting with holds some good memories, even though it does not, in itself, spark feelings of joy in you. Once you have selected the things you will be discarding, thank them before you donate, gift, or throw them in the bin. This should also be done before you start neatly arranging the items you have selected to stay.

8. You could make the day for organizing a special one

This is important, as you do not want to be disturbed or distracted while you work on decluttering your house. Instead of going on a vacation with your family, you may choose to spend the time organizing your house. This can be a really fun activity, as many have testified to. If you are married, you could talk about it with your spouse and come to an agreement. You could do the organizing with them, which is even more exciting than doing it alone. Just make sure that no other activity would clash with your decluttering.

9. Nostalgia should not be a determining factor

Even though the object that will not be discarded must inspire joy, this should not be as a result of all the years it has been with you. The fact that you used that belt in high school does not mean it must continue to remain in a box somewhere in your house. If you will never use it again, then get rid of it already! Your kids may not be as excited as you have imagined to see the make of the belt you used as a teenager. A photograph would, most likely, do.

KonMari vs Swedish Death Cleaning

When it comes to these two methods, there has been a lot of back and forth about which is the best. Although the focus of this book is on Swedish Death Cleaning, it feels appropriate to juxtapose it with KonMari. Now that we understand the way both methods are used, let us see how they measure up against each other.

1. The philosophy behind them

For KonMari, it is all about the items in the house that makes you happy and joyful. This is how you are expected to make judgments about which item stays and those that must hit the road. Swedish Death Cleaning, on the other hand, focuses on those things that must be discarded. Those using this decluttering technique are expected to envision a time when they would no longer be alive. They are to dispose of belongings that may be confusing to their loved ones when deciding on what to discard, or those embarrassing items that should not be seen by anyone else (come on, we've all got secrets).

2. How others benefit

Usually, only the person doing the decluttering benefits from using KonMari. Although you are told to stay away from decluttering the belongings of other people -including your spouse- the central focus is still on the items that bring joy to you. Looking a little closer, one might say that anyone living in the house would benefit from a house that is less cluttered and more spacious. Swedish Death Cleaning has little to do with who is cleaning up and everything to do with the friends and family of that person. The decluttering is geared at making their deaths easier on those they would leave behind. These people would not have to spend days sorting the belongings of the deceased or dealing with items that may cause a rift.

3. Clarity of message

For many who have not done thorough research on KonMari or who only flipped through the pages of the book, they might get a little confused as to what they should do with some items. There are many who, erroneously, believe that unless the item brings joy, it should be discarded. As such, they throw away things of value simply because it did not make them joyful. There is no such thing as confusion with Swedish Death Cleaning. The individual is only to discard things that have no particular value anymore and might be problematic to their loved ones once they, the person cleaning, are dead.

4. Gratitude

Marie Kondo expects all who use her technique to show appreciation to their houses and personal properties for being useful to them. They are to thank the house before they start decluttering, and also thank the items to be discarded after they have separated. Some find doing this to be weird and quirky, while others think it is liberating. With Swedish Death Cleaning, no one expects you to thank anyone or anything. The simple act of using this decluttering technique is considered to be self-sacrifice by many since the individual must put aside their own fears or worries about death and think only of making things easier on their loved ones. If anything, it is the friends and family of the individual who are often thankful.

5. The rules

This is usually what discourages many from continuing with KonMari. There are just so many strict rules to be followed, without which the person using the method cannot enjoy the full benefits.

Even after separating items that bring joy from those to be discarded, there are rules on how clothes should be folded and stored. While Swedish Death Cleaning comes with its own set of rules, they are a lot fewer and less strict. All that is expected is that you go through your belongings and be firm in your decision about the items that must go and those that will stay.

Chapter 4: Benefits of Swedish Death Cleaning

***

You may have considered all that has been said and think to yourself, this sure is a lot of work. Well, it is. In the first place, it takes a huge amount of effort (and courage) to confront the reality of your own mortality and thus make preparation for your life's end. More so, Swedish Death Cleaning is hard work. It is when you begin that you realize how much you actually own and how difficult it is to divide up what you have amongst the many people in your life. Going through every item you own and appropriately tagging them can be a tough job.

However, the prospect of the job being tough notwithstanding, Swedish Death Cleaning comes with its own benefits. These benefits far outweigh whatever stress you may go through while carrying out the task. Furthermore, it makes up for it completely.

Once you are able to get over how morbid Swedish Death Cleaning sounds and actually decide to follow through with the process, you will find out that it is one of the most wholesome practices you'd ever engage in. Swedish Death Cleaning comes with benefits you may not find anywhere else. Because of the uniqueness of the practice – decluttering your life in preparation for death – there is hardly any exercise that provides the same level of satisfaction that it brings.

Finally, before I go straight to talking about the benefits, you need to realize that Swedish Death Cleaning may not take as long as you think. This is especially so if you carry out the task over a period of time. You may not be certain of a lot of things, but one thing you can always be certain of is the fact that when you are done with the exercise, you will be glad you did. So here are some of the benefits that come from Swedish Death Cleaning.

1. It helps you manage stress

Life is stressful. This is one universal truth everyone buys into no matter where you reside or how beautiful your life is. One of the reasons people become stressed is the amount of clutter they have in their lives. When your life is filled – physically and otherwise – by items you have no further use for, the chances of you becoming stressed is high. And this often spills over to every other area of your life.

Because of how stressful life is, we are always on the lookout for ways to relieve stress and feel less overwhelmed with life. It is for this reason that individuals engage in several activities in a bid to wind down. Swedish Death Cleaning can become a tool to help you achieve this goal of living a less stressed life.

It is certain that when you live in an organized place, you will find out that your life would become less stressed. If everything is in its place and all the non-useful items either given away or put in storage, your home – and your life – would have more room thus leading to less stress.

Furthermore, it gives you fewer things to worry about, leading to an air of serenity in your immediate environment. This air of peace found around you will manifest itself and lead to serenity in your insides too. What people do not often realize is that it may be impossible to attain peace and quiet on the inside if the outside is mired in chaos.

What is being discussed here has nothing to do Yoga meditation or the like. Studies have been carried out to show that there is a connection between the level of clutter found in a person's life and how stressed they are. By extension also, if a person is stressed, their level of productivity diminishes. In a particular study carried out on housewives, it was discovered that the women who described their home spaces as being more cluttered experienced worse moods and exhibited higher signs of stress than their counterparts who had more organized homes (Saxbe & Repetti, 2009). This is exactly what Swedish Death Cleaning can help you achieve.

Finally, stress and clutter can make it difficult for your brain to function optimally. This means that it would be harder for you to engage in just one task, as opposed to when you are not stressed and when your life is uncluttered. When you engage in Swedish Death Cleaning and declutter your life, you will be less stressed, and this would eventually lead to optimal brain function.

Some of the things that cause us stress are beyond our control. However, there may come a time when you would have to take charge of your life and make sure that what stresses you, and what clutters your life, is kept within the barest minimum. In this regard, Swedish Death Cleaning is your go-to exercise.

2. It helps you deal with the fact of your mortality

We are all going to die. That is a given. Never mind whether you want to accept that or not. The fact of our own death is a reality we cannot escape from. Thus, it makes sense if we are able to confront and possibly accept this while alive. When you are in tune with the fact that your time on Earth is limited, it helps you live a more deliberate life and helps you make arrangements for what will happen at the time of your demise.

Hiding your head in the sand would not make the reality go away. Admittedly, it can be a sore subject for folks to engage in. It is at this point that Swedish Death Cleaning comes in. Swedish Death

Cleaning can be a good means to get the conversation going.

When you give up or destroy the excess stuff you have at home, it serves to bring to your notice that everything comes to an end. It makes you realize the futility in hoarding items you would have no use for eventually. This also helps you take care of other aspects of your life that may be impacted at your demise. For instance, if you have not made a will, or tidied up the paperwork for your insurance, once you begin this step, it encourages you to work on the other aspects of your life at the same time.

Furthermore, when you go through the stuff you own it reminds you who you really are. This is because the totality of a person can be summed up by the items he accumulates. Thus, when you go through and sort the items you have it would be like you staring at yourself through the lens of all you own. This would help you live in tune with who you really are. It would also help you arrange your legacy for when you will not be alive.

You must realize that at some point someone would have to take care of all of the stuff you have. It may be you or someone close to you. If you are a senior citizen, then it makes all the more sense for you to attempt to get your affairs in order as early as possible.

The truth is that if you keep putting off the time when you would arrange your properties, you may eventually never get to do it. Research has shown that people who put off cleaning eventually do not get to do it at all. In this regard, it just makes more sense to begin whatever you want to do and to start it early.

Swedish Death Cleaning also lifts the responsibility of sorting through your stuff from your family and friends. It would be wrong for you to make the assumption that others would have the time, or even be willing, to sort through your stuff at your demise. In fact, it is wrong for you to foist that responsibility on them when you can help it.

The death of a loved one can be a deeply traumatic experience and having to go through their stuff to appropriately tag them can be even more devastating. If you declutter your life and engage in Swedish Death Cleaning while you are alive, you would be showing them some kindness. It would be a way for you to help them cope with your passing when the time arrives. Decluttering while alive would also keep the memories they have of you intact. It would hardly make sense if the memories your loved ones have of you is that you left tons of unsorted stuff for them to go through. You would want to preserve the image your friends and family have of you; thus, it is needful to engage in Swedish Death Cleaning. Basically, the idea is to clean up after yourself while alive. It is the least you could do for family and friends

3. It might actually make you happy

As humans, we are in a constant search for happiness. From movies to extravagant parties and vacations, we are constantly looking for ways to live the best versions of our lives. However, it proves futile in some cases. It does appear as though life deliberately tries to make it impossible for us to be happy. It is for this reason that at every point where we find an opportunity to be happy, the advice is to grab it with both hands, regardless of how the opportunity comes.

One of the ways of achieving true happiness is through minimalism. When people own just enough stuff to keep them going each day, they tend to have less to worry about and thus are happier. Swedish Death Cleaning fits right into this minimalist philosophy. If you are a minimalist, then death cleaning is right up your alley. However, if you do not subscribe to the minimalist philosophy, or are uninterested generally in the philosophy, death cleaning would still work for you. This is because minimalist ideals have been proven to work time and again, even for people who do not subscribe to the ideology.

Again, one cardinal principle of minimalism is the idea that happiness cannot be tied to physical properties. Instead, happiness is taken to flow from the quality of the relationship one has with the people found around him. Swedish Death Cleaning opens you up to identify the things that actually matter to you. When you let go of some of the physical possessions you have hoarded over a long period, you are put in a position to better identify what matters to you and pay attention to them. This is particularly important if you engage in practice early in life. When you do so, you would better appreciate the people in your life as you grow older. You would be able to notice patterns and trends you have, and if you feel that these patterns are harmful, you can change and prepare to live a better life from that moment onwards. Although you may not be able to go into the past to correct the mistakes you have already made, you would be able to live a more fulfilled life from that moment onwards.

Additionally, people who spend a lot of time going after material possessions often end up miserable. They also find it hard maintaining relationships. Sadly, this sort of lifestyle is the one glorified by society. Even though there is ample evidence that the wanton pursuit of physical possession harms the individual more than it helps him, mainstream media and society keep promoting this sort of lifestyle and people tend to fall into these traps. Death cleaning can be like a rebellion against the established patterns in society. It is a method through which you can decide not to follow the pattern laid down by society and forge your own path.

Furthermore, it provides you happiness in another way: through giving. Decluttering often involves giving away several items that you may no longer find useful, and this comes with benefits of its own. One of these benefits is happiness to the giver because of the sense of fulfillment that comes as a result of putting smiles on the faces of others. You would not have had this experience if the items are given away on your death. When you declutter your life and give away those possessions while still alive, you are able to share in the joy of the individual receiving the items. The receiving party would also be able to express their satisfaction to you personally, and this would definitely add to the fulfillment you feel.

4. It is financially smart

While financial gains might not be topmost on your mind while you are engaging in the practice, it could be one of the benefits you can derive in the long run.

If you are strapped for cash, decluttering and selling off some of your stuff might be a smart thing to do. As a matter of fact, selling off most of your possessions would possibly be what your loved ones would do after your death. Selling them yourself gives you control over the whole process and also makes sure that the money comes to you directly while you are alive.

Also, being the owner, you would know the value of the product. This could either be the actual value of the item (i.e. the value at which you purchased it) or it could be the sentimental value of the item because of the weight you have attached to it over the years. You would be in a position to sell the item for its actual value better than any other person. Also, you have access to receipts of the items, and if you intend to sell them at auctions, it could help with tax deductions by the government.

Finally, the process can help secure the item you own while you are alive. There have been instances where caregivers disappear with properties of their host at his demise. You can make sure this isn't your plight. There are several ways of cataloging your possessions. You could even make use of technology in this regard.

There is also the option of storing the items in safe deposit boxes. When you do this, you then hand over the keys to your loved ones who would then take charge of those items at your demise.

5. Helps you organize your spending

Swedish Death Cleaning is an activity you can keep doing over and over again. It is a continuous process and not just a one-time thing. The thing is, once you begin practicing this routine and begin decluttering your life, you realize that you would no longer feel the urge to go back to the state you were in earlier. This would then mean that you would not feel the need to purchase items you would eventually have no use for. The benefit of this is that it saves you a lot of money. It redefines your spending habits and checks the urge to engage in impulse purchases.

This would also have an impact on your family because once your finances are in a good state, your family would have more money to engage in other (more important) activities. Everyone would learn how to make do with what is available.

Furthermore, if you are aged and have decided on the place where you would live out the rest of your days, Swedish Death Cleaning is important for you. Essentially, it would make sure your house is tidy and uncluttered meaning that you would have fewer things to worry about (or trip over). It is important for you to have a safe house where you do not have to worry about cleaning up and keeping track of all the million items you own. Death cleaning makes it easier for you to clean, use and live in your own home.

Techniques for Swedish Death Cleaning

First off, you have to realize that Swedish Death Cleaning is not something you could get done in a day or in one spare weekend. It involves a lot of preplanning, both mentally and physically. It is a rigorous process that may span months, although it does get easier after the first time.

Swedish Death Cleaning offers the best results when it is not seen as a one-time thing but as a type of lifestyle change. Even after the first big decluttering, you will still have to go back once in a while to check for items that have outlived their uses and give them away or sell them. This way it would be that the benefits that come to you from the procedures does not wear off after a period but last for a long time.

The first step in the process of decluttering following Swedish Death Cleaning, is gaining an understanding as to why it is important. A thorough understanding of why you want to carry out the action would help you in taking to the task with zest and fervor. It would also reveal the true nature of the practice and would be helpful when you get too tired to continue at any point.

In helping you understand why it is important, we have listed some of the benefits of the process above. You must realize that we no longer live in the era of the Vikings when a deceased person's possessions are buried with him. The practice was beneficial because it saved the living relatives the pain of having to go through the individual's property to determine what was useful and what wasn't. But most importantly, it helps them move on faster. So, when you engage in Swedish Death Cleaning, you are essentially doing it for the loved ones you would leave behind.

But apart from that, you would be doing it for yourself. As already pointed out, it is a smart way of conserving and even in some cases, generating funds. It is also a means of ensuring that the home you live in is spic and span, with everything in its place. Once you have reminded yourself of the reason for engaging in the process in the first place, the next step would be starting. So, how exactly can Swedish Death Cleaning be carried out:

1. Have a discussion with your loved ones concerning what you are doing

The first thing you should do when you are embarking in Swedish Death Cleaning is to have a frank conversation with your friends and loved ones concerning what you are doing. This could be an awkward conversation to have especially if you are getting older and death cleaning is one of the ways you are preparing for your demise. However tough it is, you just need to have the conversation. In the first place, it would help them gain perspective. It would also get their mind ready for the inevitable.

In the event that you have intentions of giving some of the property to them, having them around would be wise. They would then pick some of the items that they fancy and also help you dispose of the rest.

2. Start with the big things first

It is usually advisable that when you are engaging in death cleaning that you begin with the big items first. You may be tempted to take care of the little things such as sorting through the pictures you have gathered over the years. The idea is that if you are able to sort through the big things first, you would be better empowered to handle the little things later.

First on the list of the big things you have to take care of is furniture. Look around your home and identify the pieces of furniture that do not serve any purpose anymore. Then decide what you are going to do with them. You could give them away, donate to charity or sell them. Sometimes you might even have to give some of the items of furniture away even if they are being useful to you. This is usually in the instances where they occupy a huge space in your home, and you have other pieces of furniture that serve the exact same purpose. In that scenario, it would be wise to declutter by giving away some of that stuff.

What you should take away from here is the fact that you should begin your decluttering by focusing on the big things. The small things should be handled later. This is one of the examples where size really matters.

3. Raid your closet

People generally find it easier to go through their closet than any other aspect of their lives. It does appear as though clothes do not hold as much significance as other aspects of a person's life. When you begin with your closet you would probably do so with zeal and fervor. It would then be easier to transfer this fervor into other areas of your life.

Chances are that in your closet you have clothes that for one reason or another you haven't worn in a long period of time. Perhaps you have grown to dislike the particular outfit, or they no longer fit, or they have become so old, you should give them away.

People often say that they store properties such as items of clothing because it serves some sentimental purpose for them. This is usually said when the item of clothing was given to them by a family member or friend or loved one and this holds some significance for them. The truth, however, is that it doesn't matter the reason for which you are no longer wearing a particular item of clothing, as long as it is not in use, you should consider giving it away. Regifting a gift is an excellent way to show thoughtfulness and appreciation for the individual who had given you the gift in the first place. You would be continuing the chain and preserving the sentiment attached to the gift.

As soon as you are done decluttering you should then decide to only purchase clothes you would need them. It would make little sense to get back to the point where you were before.

4. Create a box of memories

Well, a box of memories may not be apt to describe the box, but it serves the same purpose. The box should be where you keep all of the little items which hold significance for you and which you do not want to dispose of. This box is specifically for you and no one else. Thus, at your death, the box should be destroyed. It is not a gift that can be passed on to a family member or friend.

5. Enjoy the process

You should not see death cleaning as a chore to be finished with as quickly as possible. It should be a continuous process through which you get your life together. You should learn to see it less as a task than as a way of life, one that changes your perspective about life generally. As you practice it continuously, it should make you a more generous person, more willing to give to everyone around you. It should also clamp down on the need to accumulate a lot of resources. What it should birth in you is the ability to let go of possessions easily. You would be willing to let them go as quickly as they come into your life.

You should also learn to enjoy the memories that come with the items you are working on. Even as you sort through all of your worldly possessions and probably give away a lot of them, allow yourself to savor the memories that come with each item. The memories do not certainly disappear, and you shouldn't attempt to do so with them. As the memories come, allow yourself to relive each of them again. Smile at the places that made you smile, shed a tear or two when you see the pictures of loved ones that have passed on: those are some of the benefits that come from carrying out the exercise. You should let yourself be fully immersed in the process from start to finish.

Beyond preparing your state of affairs for your demise, decluttering puts your life in order and gives it the ability to be predictable and organized. It helps you first while you are alive before helping the people you leave behind at your departure.

Applying the Techniques of Death Cleaning to Your Finances

As you put every aspect of your life together, one aspect you cannot neglect is your finances. It would be a shame if at your demise no member of your family knows your passwords or account numbers. In some cases, it may not be that you are deliberately trying to keep the information from them. It could just be that you have not been careful enough to put the information in a place where they can have easy access to it.

In a lot of instances, family and friends of an individual have to go through a lot of hassles before gaining access to the funds left by a loved one. This is very sad considering that some of these situations can be helped if the individual had taken the time to sort his affairs properly before his demise. There is the need to make adequate arrangements so that at your demise your family would have easy access to whatever funds you leave behind.

One way of solving this problem is by gathering all of the information regarding your finances into a central location. If you are worried about security and the fact that your financial information might fall into the wrong hands, then you could put the information in a secure place. It should be a place that you alone can access. This would mean that at your demise your loved ones can easily gain access to the funds left behind by you.

It is important to put down information concerning your bank, the account(s) you operate with each bank and the passwords to each account. You should also provide the details to your online banking apps, including passwords and usernames.

If you are in debt you should also make that information available. Details of any mortgage, the particular arrangement with that specific mortgage and how much you have redeemed should be listed as well.

You should also leave behind a copy of your will if you have one. Some individuals prefer to leave their wills with their lawyers. There is nothing wrong with doing that. If you choose to leave a copy of the will, be sure to leave a contact address of the lawyer who helped you prepare the will also.

Make sure to inform your family members of any insurance policy you have entered into. It isn't uncommon to find unclaimed insurance policies usually because the beneficiaries are not made aware of the policy in time. If you are currently under a life insurance policy, make sure you leave the information behind as well. If the policy you are under is the one provided by your firm then you should do well to leave behind information concerning your employers in your file for your beneficiaries to have access to.

Finally, your social information should also be stored by you upon your demise. Certainly, there are people you want to be notified about your passing, you should put down their names and contact information. You should also leave behind the passwords to your social media accounts so it would be easy for your loved ones to have access to your accounts and notify every one of your demise when the time eventually comes.

Other Decluttering Techniques

Some people believe that Swedish Death Cleaning is too morbid and makes them uncomfortable. They believe in the need to declutter and sort out their lives but do not agree with the death cleaning process laid out to do so. If you are one such person, it is okay. There are several other techniques you can employ to declutter your life and create space for the really important stuff. Apart from Swedish Death Cleaning, some of the equally effective methods that exist include:

- **Packing party:** This method is not for the fainthearted. This method can only be applied if you are really serious about decluttering. You should also consider going through with this method if you are already packing to leave a particular apartment within a period of time.

It usually involves a great deal of preparation before you even begin. Also, the extent of the work you have to do might make it necessary that you employ the help of others. Family and friends can step in to help you with this process because it can be overwhelming if you decide to engage in it alone.

The method works this way: you gather all you own and put them into boxes as though you are moving. Then begin making use of the products you need from the boxes. After a period, you would discover that there would be items left in the boxes which you have not made use of in a long while. Those are the ones you should give away, or at least consider giving away once the time comes.

The amount of work required for this method is justified by the benefits it brings. The party packing method guarantees that you would get rid of all you are not currently using. It will also be great for you if you are moving because what you just have to do is to move to your new house with the boxes you have been using. You would then give away the boxes that you have had no use for.

As stated earlier, this method works best if you were already planning to move which means that you would not have to spend resources on boxes or expend energy packing up just to declutter. This method may also be problematic if you do not have friends and family to pitch in to make the task easy for you.

- **Practice giving away one thing per day**: This practice was made popular by Colleen Madsen. He suggests that this would work well for people who may not have the time to go through death cleaning once and so want to take it a day at a time. The idea is that by giving away your possessions one day at a time you would eventually achieve the same result you would if you carried out the death cleaning in one fell swoop.

This method helps incorporate decluttering into your lifestyle. When you carry out the act of giving away one possession, one day at a time, you would not necessarily need a specific time in your life to declutter, it would become a routine you engage in every day. This system also allows you to create your own routine. You can decide to either give away a lot of things or to just give away something small each day. This flexibility makes it that you would be able to do so much because you would not be inhibited by procedures laid down by others.

This system requires a level of consistency from you. If you are going to tow this path then you have to be sure that you would have the time, zeal and energy to follow through when you start. You would have to consider your schedule; the amount of work you do each day and the time you have left to yourself at the end of each day. Although giving away one possession each day may appear like an easy thing to do, it isn't as simple as it sounds. You have to first determine the items to give away, how you would give them away and to whom. All of these would take considerable time and energy.

Finally, this may not work for you if you are not a methodical person willing to follow through with a process. If you are more given to accomplishing a huge task over a limited period than following through a task over a given period of time, then this system may not work well for you.

- **Make a list**: This suggestion on decluttering was offered by Dana Myers. She teaches that in trying to declutter, you should first discover the areas you believe you want to work on and make a list of them. You could either decide to make a list beginning from the easiest areas to the hard areas or in the reverse. What should inform how you carry out the cleaning is what areas of your life you really want to sort out and for how long you want to do it.

- **Try the Oprah Winfrey Closet Method**: This method is named after Oprah Winfrey although it did not originate with her. She was just the person who made it very popular. She first talked about it as the method she uses to discover items of clothing that she does not use often and thus would want to give away. She has stated that it has worked for her for a long time and has called on other individuals to follow her lead.

According to the practice, one is supposed to hang the clothes in their closet facing a reverse direction. Then as they wear the clothes, they would put them back facing the right direction. The effect of this is that eventually, it would only be the clothes facing the right direction that have been used over time. It would give you an idea of the clothes you wear frequently and the ones you do not wear at all. Chances are that you can do without the ones you seldom wear so it is advisable to give those away.

One of the benefits of this method is that it is relatively easy and does not require a lot to begin. Furthermore, almost anyone can follow this method the type of job/income/personal proclivities notwithstanding. You can use this method for a variety of other household items. It will show you the stuff you own that are just occupying space and cluttering your life and thus you would have to give them up. If you decide to use than for other items apart from clothes, then you have to devise a means of marking the ones you have used and the ones you haven't.

This method requires a lot of discipline. You would have to be deliberate about putting the clothes exactly the way you are meant to. Any mistake here could muddle up the process and at the end, you would not have a clear idea of the clothes frequently worn and the ones that aren't. Again, this method works best for clothing. It may be difficult to apply the method to other areas of one's life because of the difficulty in determining the way to mark what is useful and what isn't.

Finally, this method will not work if you do not use the items frequently. If the items you want to sort are the things you only make use of once in a while, then it might not be wise for you to follow the process

- **Try the four-box method:** This is also one of the great minimalist ways of decluttering your life. The four-box method is a system where you get four boxes and label them: trash, give away, relocate and keep.

These boxes should be kept in each room of your house and should not be moved. At any point when you decide to sort through the stuff in any room of your house, you sort them according to the boxes. You are to make sure that every item you pick up fits into one of the boxes. Do not pass over any item or keep it aside because you could not find an appropriate box for them. Furthermore, the things you keep should not be greater than the ones you want to give away. In fact, the reverse is supposed to be the case, or in any case, they could be the same.

There is another version of this decluttering method where the box for relocate is replaced with undecided. In this method, you can decide to put the items you are not sure about into the last box. That way you will not give away or dispose of items that would be useful to you later on in the future. It also allows you to revisit the box and then make a decision on what you want to do with the items found therein.

The four-box method is so great because it offers you flexibility and the ability to take things slowly and at your own pace. You would only get to declutter an aspect of your life once you are satisfied it is something you want to do.

However, you should be careful to make sure that the undecided box does not become too full and becomes problematic for you. The box should not be used as a means of putting off making decisions concerning an item. It should be used when you have already made the decision to leave it for a later date or when you believe that although the item may not be serving you at the moment, it would serve you in the future.

The method states that instead of going through the process of discovering which items you have to give away, instead, you focus on the ones you want to keep and then decide on what you would do to the rest of the items. The process entails going through everything you have own before you decide on the ones to keep or the ones to give away. For instance, if you own a number of shirts, you could gather them together, then go through each one m, one shirt at a time, before making a decision. You do not skip any item of clothing. You take the time to go through the process for every item till you come to the decision of what you want to keep and what you want to give away.

This process is beneficial because it is thorough. You are not in danger of overlooking anything at all. It focuses on a particular category of item, and sorts through them entirely. It helps you weed out items that you have duplicates of and can be a great way of sorting out multiple areas of your life at the same time.

However, this method is time-consuming and is not ideal if you want to do quick work.

Chapter 5: Some Myths on Decluttering

***

What exactly are decluttering myths? They can be described as things that hinder your decluttering activities. Some of them cause people to keep clutter in their homes or offices for months and even years. It is something that does not allow you to start your decluttering plan talk more of finishing it. A lot of people can relate to most of these myths, but if you want to declutter your space effectively, this should not be an issue at all.

There are a lot of those myths out there; some are even yet to be discovered. Some of the common ones include the following:

The Clutter Is Overwhelming

Decluttering is not as easy as it sounds. It is extremely tough, especially when you have a lot of clutter in your space. This is probably one of the first myths that discourage people from finishing their decluttering plan.

When you walk into a room full of clutter, you might get discouraged because of the size of the mess. Some people are completely disoriented at first sight of their clutter during decluttering when we all know that they are the primary cause of the clutter in the first place. This myth is probably one of the most feared amongst others.

The Hassle of Getting Rid of the Clutter

This myth and the first are almost the same. But the main

difference is that this has to do with the removal of the clutter. The first one deals with starting the decluttering plan in the first place. This myth also discourages a lot of people because how will you declutter your home when you don't know how to get rid of the clutter properly? People with this problem can start their decluttering plan but stop at a point because they have no proper way of disposing of their clutter.

The Clutter Will Still Come Back

If you are planning to declutter your home and you have this mindset, you are not going anywhere. Because how can you aspire to progress but desire to fail. When you always think that your clutter will come back, what exactly is the reason to declutter in the first place? Just like keeping fit, after you have lost a lot of pounds, you must keep fit. After decluttering your space, you must keep it decluttered at all times. If you put in an enormous amount of effort to declutter a space, I don't think you would want your efforts to go to waste.

Sentimental Value Attached to Some Things

This is another old myth. This is one that does not allow the progress of decluttering. You might think it's little, but it's probably one of the toughest myths to date. Some people are scared of decluttering and getting rid of a lot of stuff because they are not able to let go of something because of its sentimental value or the memories attached to it as the case may be.

Thinking That Your Clutter Is Far from A Big Deal

When you think that your clutter is not a big deal, you would not have any zeal to start your decluttering plan. This is just you sitting and looking at your clutter, thinking that it has no effect on you or anything that you do. But bad news, clutter causes diseases and different illnesses. It also causes anxiety. You can never really be comfortable in a house that has clutter. Like it or not, clutter has a way of changing the mood and feeling of a particular person. It is advised that you get rid every kind of clutter in your home because it makes you healthy.

Thinking That Your Clutter Is All Worthless Garbage

Your clutter may consist of a lot of things such as sweaters, trousers, shoes, and many more. Instead of throwing them away because you think they are garbage, those items could be sold online or in a yard sale. You could even recycle some of the clutter or use them for something more creative. The aim here is making good money off something you consider as garbage.

Not Having A Right Way to Store Your Clutter

This is also a fascinating myth. Many people would want to start this decluttering exercise but don't know where to store their extra items. Sometimes it's good to store them in hidden cupboards that is, if you must keep them. And you could also get plastic containers that could help you in distinguishing and organizing your clutter based on importance. You could buy a plastic foldable wardrobe that you could use to keep clothes that you don't want to throw away — clothes like a wedding dress.

Fearing That You May Need the Things You Throw Away Later

Another reason why people fear decluttering. Some people say that they like the exact way everything in their house is. They never want it to change even a little, because according to them, they use everything exactly the way it is. This is one of the main causes of clutter in a home. Not wanting to put everything the way it is because you believe that it is exactly fine the way you left it. Then you end up putting more and more and more and just like that, you are creating clutter. These types of people do not want to declutter because they fear that they might need those things again sometime in the future, so what do they do? They leave the mess precisely like that.

Keeping Things Because They Are Gifts

This also falls under sentiments, but it is one of the reasons why you have useless junk in your house. It might be coffee mugs, napkins, old shoes, and so much more. Things that the people who gave them to you probably never remember existed. Sometimes you should look at how it affects your health in every aspect before thinking of others. Would you rather be anxious all the time in your life? Or would you rather be comfortable like every normal person in a decluttered house?

Having the Feeling That Some Things in Your Clutter Connect You with The Past

Clutter does not in any way connect you with the past except if you used to live in a junkyard. Connect with the past by using pictures and scrapbooks like every other person. If you need that clutter so badly in your life, you could take a picture of it and then send it on its merry way to holy trash heaven. This clutter is not helping you in any way, especially if it is in your home. You must organize it for you to have an excellent, healthy, and comfortable lifestyle all the days of your life.

These myths, as we all know, are the things that hinder people from focusing more on the goal of completing their decluttering plan. These myths make people focus on the hard process of decluttering rather than the result, which is the satisfaction of having a decluttered space. But the real question is, how exactly do we handle these myths? What can we do to prevent them from poisoning our minds?

It's straight forward. All you have to do is to set a goal and know the importance of getting to that goal. For instance, if you have a thirty-day decluttering work plan in mind, all you have to do to get there is to focus on the benefits of a decluttered space when you are done. When you can completely and effectively focus on all the benefits you would get from a decluttered space, you would never want to have clutter around you anymore. Just the thought of it may not only scare but utterly disgust you.

Chapter 6: How to Overcome the Fear of Dying

***

The fear of death is a phenomenon that is common among a lot of people today. It is admittedly higher with old folks because of the fact that they are almost at the end of their lives, however, the fear is found among people of various ages and classes and creeds.

There are two classes of the fear of death or dying. In the first category, there are people who are afraid of dead things and dead bodies. This category of people cannot go near a dead body and cannot be around items associated with death such as graveyards, coffins, etc. Usually, this fear of dead things brings with it an irrational obsession with death and all things dead. This phenomenon is known as necrophobia – a term coined from two Greek words necro (death) and phobia (fear).

Some of the symptoms of necrophobia are an unhealthy obsession with death, an often-debilitating fear of dead things, headaches and migraines, etc. Necrophobia is usually traceable to a particular incident in the individual's life. It is not uncommon to find out that the individual had an experience in his life that he had not been able to fully manage, hence the fear of death.

On the other hand, there is thanatophobia. This disorder is similar to necrophobia except that this time the person is not afraid of dead things but is afraid of dying himself. They may manifest the same symptoms as a person suffering from necrophobia, so it is possible to find out that a person suffering from thanatophobia has a fear of coffins and funerals and dead bodies too. But as already stated, this fear is not projected outwards but inwards. The fear could also manifest as the fear of being buried and cremated.

Symptoms of thanatophobia include physical symptoms such as dizziness and frequent panic attacks – here the individual usually experiences a loss of control of his life, fluctuations in temperature, illness, anxiety disorders – this time the individual is afraid of falling ill and does all to avoid this happening to him. Thanatophobia has also been linked with other phobias. For instance, it is not uncommon to find that a person who suffers from thanatophobia would have other phobias such as fear of snakes, spiders, etc. It may also include non-physical symptoms such as when a person goes through great lengths to maintain their youth, an obsession with the way they could die and the feeling that one is about to get choked.

Information concerning the cause of thanatophobia is not as scanty as the information regarding necrophobia. A lot of research has been carried out into the phenomenon in order to discover its origins and causes. Some of the symptoms may not be common among everyone but there are specific signs that usually indicate that a particular person is most likely suffering from thanatophobia. These markers are known as risk factors and usually include the following:

Age: Research has revealed that young persons may be more likely to suffer from death anxiety than older persons. Generally, it is found that people who are old often have the fear of the dying process and not of death itself while it is the young persons who are afraid of dying and death. The only exception to this rule is that women over 50 are more likely to fear death and the effects of the death of their loved ones on them and everything around them than men.

Traumatic Events: A traumatic event early in the life of a person may predispose the person to have an irrational fear of death and dying later in life. The sort of traumatic event that could trigger thanatophobia later in life is usually a near-death experience. For instance, an individual who has had an accident may likely develop thanatophobia if adequate therapy is not provided the individual.

Health Challenges: A person who has had recurrent physical health challenges may experience anxiety regarding death and dying. This is because having come close to death multiple times, he would be scared of eventually going over the edge.

How to Take Care of Thanatophobia

If you are suffering from thanatophobia, you should know that it is more common than you realize and also that there are certain steps you can take to handle it. Here are a few suggestions:

Look for Professional Help

A lot of individuals try to take care of this particular phobia on their own. This move usually stems from the ill-conceived idea that thanatophobia is something mild and thus would not require the assistance of a professional. If you are thinking along this line you are terribly wrong. Every phobia has physical, emotional and mental ties. This means that you are likely to fall into error and exacerbate the problem if you attempt to take care of it on your own.

You should know that a lot of the individuals who have successfully overcome this phobia did so with the help of a licensed therapist who guided them through the process from start to finish. Gaining access to a professional is not tedious. There are several online forums where you can request and be provided a professional to help you.

You should be mindful when requesting a professional. You have to ask for one specific to your needs. There are a lot of licensed professionals cutting across different areas. While requesting help, ensure that the person you eventually get connected to is suited for your particular needs.

Therapy Might Work for You

There are several of them open to anyone suffering from the fear of death. The first is Cognitive Behavioral Therapy (CBT). This mode of treatment has proven effective for use in the treatment of depression and various forms of phobias. It would also work for thanatophobia because at the moment anxiety related to the fear of dying has not been categorized distinctly.

The treatment seeks to provide practical ways of handling the phobia. During the sessions, the individual would be required to discuss their fears and come to terms with them. They may also be taken to the specific places that increase their anxiety and, in this way, they would be forced to confront their fears and overcome them.

Techniques for relaxation would also be taught to the individuals during this procedure. Relaxation techniques are important because the individual would need to handle their fears through relaxation whenever they feel triggered. Some of the relaxation techniques include deep breaths, focus trainings and even meditations. Part of the relaxation techniques taught would include the teachings about the necessity of rest for the overall health and comfort of the individual. He would also be admonished about his diet and how the food he eats could have an impact on his mental health.

Medications may also be prescribed by the professional (this is one of the reasons why it is important that the individual offering the help be a professional). Individuals who suffer from depression often are prescribed antidepressants and beta blockers to help them manage their anxiety.

The technique that usually works best is a combination of medications and therapy. However, it is not ideal for the medication to be taken over a long period of time. This is because such a move would lead to overdependence on the drugs and might cause the individual to become an addict. The individual is expected to focus on the therapy and eventually changing it to a coping mechanism any time the anxiety from the episodes arises.

Adopt Rituals/Try Being Spiritual

You may not feel like following this especially if you are not a religious person. However, one thing you must never forget is the fact that rituals can help make you feel as though there is a meaning to life. They let you believe that there is a reason for life and existence. The same goes for religion and spirituality.

In fact, there are studies that show that people of faith – those who believe in a higher power or follow the tenets of a specific religion – do not typically suffer from the fear of death and dying. Most religions have an explanation for life, death and what happens in the afterlife. Most of the anxiety that usually surrounds the fear of death stems from the fact that a lot of people do not know what would happen to them once they die. Any religion you subscribe to would definitely help in that regard.

However, if you find that you cannot stomach the idea of subscribing to any religion you could simply develop some rituals that you could follow. It need not be something elaborate. It could be something as simple as writing in your journal each day, chronicling your life and experiences. You could also decide to take periodic walks etc.

Prepare for Your Passing

At no point will be the thoughts of death entirely disappear. What the therapist would seek to achieve is a situation where the thoughts of death would not be debilitating for you. The idea is to live a full life to the point where death would no longer faze you.

Another reason for the cause of the fear of death is the fact that the individuals often feel out of control of their lives. The anxiety stems from the fact that although the individual knows that death is an eventuality, he cannot know when exactly it will occur. One of the ways of taking back control is through making adequate preparations for your passing.

Making preparations for your passing includes making a will and designating a power of attorney. The individual who has your power of attorney can make decisions for you at the time of your death. They would be the ones to carry out whatever last wish you were not able to conclude. It would be reassuring for you knowing that at your passing whatever wishes you have would be wrapped up by someone else.

You can also plan your memorial service while alive. This has become a common practice amongst a lot of people. In your plan you could include whether you would like to be cremated or buried. You could also decide the seemingly trivial things such as the outfit you want to be buried in, the number of persons that would be at your funeral and even the songs that would be played.

This will certainly take the pressure off of your loved ones as they would not be in doubt as to what you actually want to be done for you at your passing.

CHAPTER 7: DECLUTTERING GUIDE, A 10-MINUTE DAILY ROUTINE

***

This guide is written to assist you with a structure for your decluttering. It will last for a period of 30 days and every activity, for each day, can be done in, give or take, ten minutes. Remember that with Swedish Death Cleaning, you want to keep those things that would be of use to your family or any other person you may wish to bequeath a particular item.

To achieve anything, you must have step-by-step goals to your final objective. Without them, you are likely to get sidetracked and revert to old habits. This is why this chapter is so important. It keeps you focused and also ensures you are not tempted to try organizing everything in every room on a single day. The checklist in Chapter 9 should be used along with this guide to mark your daily accomplishments.

1st Week

Milestone: the goal for this week is for you to gain the needed momentum that will carry you throughout your 30-day journey of decluttering your home. By the end of this week, you should have organized your shelves, pockets, books, foods, and your kids' toys. The floors in your house should also be free of those little things that have either been used up or were not returned to their rightful place.

Day 1: begin this thirty-day challenge with the small stuff. The first day should be basic, yet meaningful. Clean out your house by picking up whatever trash is on the floor in the living room, kitchen, bedroom, porch, lawn, and so on. Load up your trash bag and dispose appropriately. Make sure that there are no used-up items left lying about at the end of this first day.

Day 2: look for the little things that you often use, but which may be out of their designated place. Such items may include toothbrushes, pencils, and the like. Have a box ready for the things you would like to give to certain people and one for donations. Now, after you have arranged those little things in their place, put into the appropriate boxes that which you would prefer to gift to a friend or family member, and those you would like to donate. The rest should be thrown in the trash bag.

Day 3: your shelves and any other surface where you keep things are next in line. If the items here are for decorative purposes, keep those that inspire some positive emotion in you or those that have not deteriorated with time. The rest, you may take a picture of but must discard in either of the boxes you have set aside or put them in the trash bag. If the items are useful for much more than to be displayed, then discard those you have no intention of ever using again.

Day 4: your pockets. How many times have you, while washing your clothes or going through them, found something of interest from a while back? This could be money, paper on which you wrote a phone number, important receipts, etc. Search the pockets of every clothing item that you have worn and that still hangs from your wardrobe. In keeping with the motive behind Swedish Death Cleaning, you do not want your friends or family members to find something you would rather have taken to the grave with you. As such, search the pockets meticulously and discard items as you choose.

Day 5: when was the last time you checked your packaged foods to ascertain if they are close to or past their expiration dates? Do that today. Check your refrigerator and every other food storage space for those things you and your family will no longer consume for whatever reason. If you would like to give out those that are still edible, then do so. Dispose of what is left appropriately. You may also use this time to replace those foods that have been depleted or expired. Also, organize your foods neatly.

Day 6: arrange your books. You know those old paperbacks that you have not touched in years (and, probably, will not touch in more years to come), how about keeping a soft copy instead. See if there are eBook versions of those books. If you found them, then give the books out. Some libraries or bookstores will, very likely, appreciate the gesture. You could also give them to your kids or anyone that has asked for them or you know would love them. You can also handle newer books in this way, if you know you may not read them anytime soon. Keep those few books that are left in a neat order.

Day 7: if you have little kids, then there is every possibility that their rooms are littered with toys. Maybe they play with the toys in your room and have strewn them in several corners. While you may have to talk to them afterwards about keeping their things in order, you should pick them all up and return them to their usual spot. You may get a box, label it toys, and arrange the playthings into it. If you do not have kids, then you can take a break today and appreciate all that you have done and how much clutter is gone already.

Do not forget to check your pockets carefully, as some things may be very small and inconspicuous. If foods are too close to their expiration dates (say, two weeks or less), dispose of them.

Weekly checklist.

	Week One	I picked up everything that wasn't disposed or arranged correctly and organized them. I also decluttered the shelves, food, my books, and the pockets of my clothes.

Next week, most of the focus will be on the bedrooms in your house. Remember to ask for permission before entering anybody's bedroom (even if it's your kids') or discarding items that do not belong to you. The second week should be even more fun

2nd Week

Milestone: it's time to really get into it. This week, much of your focus should be on the bedrooms. You will be decluttering everything from furniture you would like to see go and the items underneath beds which no longer serve any particular purpose. You will also be decluttering the items in your drawers and your accessories. The goal is to clean up the room where you often wake up and, from here, to move on to other rooms.

Day 8: look around the bedroom(s), if you see some furniture that you, and whoever you share them with, have always wanted to give out or just throw away, this is the right time to do so. Also, there might be items around the house that simply exist for decorative purposes but no longer serve you in the same way. That is to say, you no longer find them aesthetically pleasing. Discard these also. Just remember to ask the permission of whoever owns these properties or that share them with you before discarding

Day 9: now it gets a bit tougher. Today, you'll be decluttering your wardrobe. True, some clothes may bring back memories of the good times you had, but you must act decisively. The main objective of this activity is to have a home with less stuff in it. So, take out those clothes you are quite sure you won't be putting on anytime soon, or ever again. Send some out, if you will, as donations to churches or charity organizations.

Day 10: clear out your bedside table and office desk. The same routine follows; if there are items you no longer have need for, discard them appropriately. Also, you may discard items that you feel your family should not be bothered with after your death. Some items may be stored elsewhere, besides the top of these tables in your bedroom. Only keep those things that hold some kind of value, and that you make use of everyday. You may set a limit for how much should be displayed on the office desk, vanity, bedside table, and so on. Five to six items should be enough.

Day 11: open your drawers and take out all the contents. Now separate them into different categories. Those you have not worn in over a year but are still good quality and style, should be kept in one pile. Those you wear frequently should be arranged in another pile. While those you would be tossing in the trash should be in another pile. Now you can, neatly, arrange those ones you frequently wear back into the drawer. I'm sure you know what to do with the other two piles. There may be more than just undergarments in your drawers. Treat them in the same manner.

Day 12: This week, most of the focus will be on the bedrooms in your house. Start with checking beneath the beds in every room of the house. If your kids are young adults, then it might be necessary to ask their permission before decluttering their rooms or invading their space, as they may see it. Also, before disposing of things that are not yours, remember to ask the permission of the owner, whether it's a spouse, partner, roommate, or kids. For your own belongings, discard those things you forgot were still in your possession and have no need for anymore.

Day 13: make room for those items that, although hold some value now or will in the future, seem to have no particular place in your home. Since you can't just leave them lying about, here are some solutions:

1. Put them in a box and shove it under your bed. This is mostly done for those items that may be valuable in the future or have sentimental value now.

2. Keep them in an empty drawer. Usually, this is done for items that you will make use of presently and frequently.

Day 14: your hats, bracelets, wristwatches, sunglasses, and other accessories also need to be decluttered. Keep only those you will continue to wear and discard the rest in the manner you must have gotten used to by now. Also, tidy up your shoes today. Those you will not toss but need to be repaired, keep them aside. Clean your shoes and arrange them neatly. Those that need to be fixed, do so and decide whether you will donate or keep using them.

Do not forget to request permission before entering the bedroom of anyone besides yours. Check carefully beneath your bed.

Weekly Checklist

	Week Two	With the consent of all concerned, I've fully decluttered the bedrooms. I made room for items which do not have a permanent place and organized my accessories.

How cool was this week? Now, your bedroom is all cleaned up and organized. Take a look at the rooms you have decluttered. How much has changed? Next week, you'll be organizing your kitchen, office supplies, holiday decorations, cleaning supplies, wine cabinet, and rugs. More adventure ahead.

3rd Week

Milestone: they say the kitchen is the heart of every home. This week, you will surgically declutter your kitchen and ensure it keeps beating in top shape. The equipment you often use in cleaning you home, also needs to be cleaned. You will take off holiday decorations that are past their season and keep or discard them. You will also organize your office supplies, towels and rugs, and —if you have any— your pets' toys.

Day 15: the kitchen is an essential part of any house and this week, you should concentrate on decluttering and tidying it. When decluttering, you may discover that you have one too many pots or plates or spoons. When you find such excessive duplicate items, determine which should be donated, given to friends and family or sold in a garage sale. The latter is another effective method of discarding items you have no use for anymore. This should also be done for the Tupperware. Discard duplicates and those without containers or lids. Some kitchen utensils may also be damaged. If they cannot be repaired, then toss them in the trash.

Day 16: they say that the longer spirits stay in a cabinet, the better they taste, but most times people keep empty bottles of wine or rum on their cabinets, and it takes up space. You may look at your cabinets and wonder why there's no space; you should know that the problem is from you. If you need the bottles for something important, you can store them somewhere else. If not, throw them away or recycle them. Some people go online looking for that kind of bottles to purchase. You can easily make money from your empty bottles.

Day 17: a lot of people don't know how to keep their cleaning supplies and equipment. They are not clothes that should be folded with every use. Any time you are done cleaning, try to throw away the empty containers and other equipment that you might never use ever again. Your cleaning supplies cabinet or drawers should be clean. You should not need to search for everything like a mad person before you find them. Make life easier for yourself by decluttering your cleaning supplies and equipment.

Day 18: this might seem irrelevant, but pets' toys and other supplies can cause clutter. It may seem unimportant, but it could cause unnecessary mess in your home. When you get your pet a new toy, and you notice that he or she already has a lot more, try and get rid of the old ones, especially the ones that you know that he or she would never play with again. Those things are just there to create clutter in your home. You could sell them to other people with pets (that's if they are still in good condition), if not just throw them away. I don't think they are going to be missed that much.

Day 19: whether it's decorations from Christmas, Easter, Halloween, or even Saint Patrick's Day, these decorations are probably stacked somewhere in the house taking up unnecessary space. Some of which you have used just once. Some that you will never use, some of them are not even in good shape anymore. Sort them out and throw them away. Keep the decorations that you will use.

Day 20: office supplies are among those things in every house that are frequently without any form of order. You may be thinking, "but I do not have an office in my house." But your notepads, envelopes, stapler, pens, and stamps are office supplies. If you find some missing from where you, usually, return them, then you should check your kitchen, living room, entryway, and so on. You just might find then there. Do away with those you no longer want or need and arrange what is left. Keep them in a place that is easily accessible and resolve to become committed to returning each of them after use.

Day 21: it's probably high time you replaced towels and rugs. Some may only need to be washed, but there may be those ones which are torn in some areas or have faded from being used for such a long period. Throw out those worn-out towels and rugs and wash those which only need to be cleaned.

Do not forget to neatly arrange your decorative items somewhere. Don't throw them all out, as you might need them next holiday.

Weekly Checklist

	Week Three	I organized my office supplies, decorations, cleaning supplies, wine cabinet, and kitchen.

How's that for exciting, right? I'm sure you handled this week well. Don't beat yourself up if you feel you missed anything. You're a champion already, and you are almost at the end of this journey. Next week you'll go into your bathrooms and declutter them. You'll also deal with cluttered emails and DVDs. Ride on.

4th Week

Milestone: you weren't going to leave your bathroom out, were you? This week, you'll be dealing with expired medication, your computer files, emails, DVDs and CDs, and your physical mail.

Day 22: let us begin today as a continuation of last week. There are some meds in the bathroom which need to be taken care of. If you have a lot of medications and medical supplies that you don't use anymore, you need to arrange them and sort them based on importance. And most importantly you should check their expiry date before throwing them away because if they are not yet expired, they can still be handy. But if they are expired drugs, you need to throw them out immediately because if you keep them in your house, a friend or even your kids could take them and end up critically endangering his or her life. So, try and save a life by throwing away expired medications or medical supplies.

Day 23: decluttering your home goes to even the most unlikely places. Some people have a lot of DVDs and CDs that they no longer watch or listen to. Some of them from the 80s or even the 90s just sitting there doing nothing but gathering dust and making a place look very untidy. You have to clear out all the CDs and DVDs that you don't watch or will never watch again. You could give them to people who would watch them, sell them online, or throw them away. You can make some money from your old tapes when you sell them online.

Day 24: computer files can also cause clutter. You can have a lot of files in your laptop that you never thought were there. Files that have no use nor importance to you. This may take a long while, but all you have to do is to carefully sort out all your files based on relevance. Then delete the files that have little or no importance. When you do this, try to refresh your computer memory, and you will find out that your computer will run smoothly and more effectively because having a lot of files on your computer only slows it down.

Day 25: the nightstand is an unusual place to find clutter, but it does exist. The clutter might consist of all sorts of things. The priority now is to select the things you don't want there anymore carefully. Come to think of it; your nightstand is supposed to consist of an alarm clock, a lamp and probably your mobile phone. Any other things on top of your nightstand are just there to reduce the available space.

Day 26: you could probably do this last because many people get sentimental about throwing away old pictures because of specific memories they want to keep. But if you have photos that you have no use for, you must throw them away. And it might be a better idea to do this when the feeling of excitement is still relatively high and you're a lot more decisive. Some albums may consist of landscape or even animals (that's if you are a photographer) and we all know that they might not be used at all. So why keep stuff that is just there to create clutter and to reduce space? Or better still, you could use them for decorations.

Day 27: yes, emails can also cause clutter in your computer or mobile phones. The question is, what exactly are you doing with emails from 10 years ago? Nothing. Clear them out, sort them by relevance.

After doing that, delete the emails that have little or no significance. After doing that, you will notice that your email inbox will look better and more interactive and accessible. You might have three email accounts, and this method should apply to all of them. This would also create more space for you to receive more essential emails instead of harboring the unimportant ones.

Day 28: regular mail, yes, the ones that come directly to your doorstep have been known to cause unnecessary clutter in the home. When you receive a lot of mail, be it bills, invitations, invoices and so on, you should learn to sort them out immediately when they arrive on your doorstep. Because when you leave them somewhere and only attend to the important ones, the unimportant ones begin to cause clutter, and that's far from being ok. But if the mail has gotten to the point that it looks like a big heap of newspaper, you should recycle the paper.

Do not forget to check the trash icon on your computer to permanently delete certain files. Instead of deleting some email, you can archive them if they will be important for future reference.

Weekly Checklist

	Week Four	I went through my emails, physical mail, other computer files, pictures, DVDs, and medication, and completely decluttered them.

Just two more days to go. You've truly come a long way. Go through your house and call yourself a champ, it's well deserved. The final week is not much work, but it is just as vital as all the preceding activities. You'll be putting some things in place to ensure you don't have to declutter your house in such a major way again

5th Week

Milestone: the goal of this week is to put systems in place that will guarantee sustainability. You'll have to purchase waste bins and deal with whatever clutter is outside your house but still within your property.

Day 29: the final days should be dedicated to activities that would help sustain the order you have achieved. Make sure there is a waste bin close to every room. You could also give the kids a box for when they have something they would like to donate or throw out. They could also use this box to store things they will not use for some time.

Day 30: there tends to be more clutter outside of most houses than indoors. Pick up all that is outside and put the items where they should be (which could also be the trash bag). Clean whatever is dirty and is still good enough to be used. This would prevent clutter from getting into the house, ruining all your hard work over the past 29 days.

Do not forget to label the boxes you give your kids according to their names and the function of each box.

Weekly Checklist

	Week Five	I found waste bins for every room in my house, gave boxes to my kids to help them continue decluttering their stuff and organized the clutter outside my house.

You really are a hero. Go ahead and take all the pictures you want. You set your heart to it, and you accomplished your objective. You can now enjoy your clutter-free home.

Chapter 8: Declutter Your Mind

***

Your mind is the base of operations for every action or inaction you'll ever take. This is where your potential for success and ability to keep going, despite the odds, is decided. Choosing to declutter your home usually seems right and easy at first, but many find it to be a daunting challenge once they get into it. After the first week, some just want to give up entirely and return to their normal routine. This is because, having a mind that is filled with clutter, the individual would be unable to stay focused. Many people tend to worry about the outcome of everything, especially those outside of their control. A cluttered mind would constantly nag at you and create the impression that you have so much to do in so little time. With about 60,000 thoughts running through the mind of an average person each day, it is easy to see how discouraging it can be when the majority of those thoughts are centered on negativity, impossibility, and when they keep replaying in a person's head.

For these reasons, decluttering one's mind can be really helpful in keeping a person consistent, dedicated, and, ultimately, productive. These tips below can assist you with accomplishing just that. Try them out, and see your headspace become less cluttered and more organized.

Try Meditation

This usually works, almost immediately, to help people focus their thoughts. Unlike what many believe about meditation, it does not, necessarily, have to connote some type of spirituality. It really is all about getting control of your mind, and making it stay in the present. It is also one activity that requires practice in order to be perfected. The more time you can carve out of your, probably, busy schedule to spend meditating, the easier it becomes to stay still for longer and longer periods doing nothing but meditating. When you meditate, you may choose to focus on your breathing; as it rises and falls. It is not compulsory for your eyes to be closed, but if it would be distracting to leave them open, then keep them shut. Most people are usually more concerned about which pose they should take while meditating. But this is not more important than the place you meditate. It should be quiet and with few distractions. Abandon every worrying thought and imagination and think only of your breath or heartbeat. As you do so, your pulse will become less frantic, as opposed to when you restlessly go about your daily activities with a cluttered mind.

Have a Routine for Most Things

Whether we've given any thought to it or not, we all have those activities in our lives that are essential to our effectiveness and are repetitive. We cannot be expected to be productive should we skip them, but they take up unnecessary mental space and nag at us until we have completed them. If you recognize them as routine, you can place these activities on autopilot mode. Instead of thinking and worrying about doing them, you just get right on it without much mental energy being expended. These things may include having to brush your teeth in the morning, bathing, choosing the clothes to wear, making your bed, and deciding on what to eat. Even at work, you can place some activities on autopilot. If you do certain things repeatedly, then they will become one less thing you fuss over.

This is not to say that you should write down such routines. Maybe you should write down what you will have for breakfast, lunch, and dinner on different days. But it is unnecessary to write about having to brush your teeth in the evening or putting your computer on in the office. Also, while it is good to have routines, leave some room for spontaneity.

Refuse Negativity

What you dwell on in your mind, is, often, what is manifested in your reality. You can attract failure to your life by belittling your abilities in your thoughts, because it will be near impossible for you to find the drive to keep pushing against the barriers on your way to success. For many people, the negative thoughts they have far outweigh the positive. And they wonder why they are unproductive and unsuccessful in any venture. While you are not encouraged to be proud, you should be emotionally intelligent enough to recognize your strengths and be thankful for them. Know that, in all the world, there is no other person quite like you. For this reason, pursue self-development and be the best you can possibly strive for. Instead of letting fear hold you from taking an action, critically analyze the potential risks of any venture and decide whether or not to continue. Look at yourself in the mirror and appreciate yourself for all of life's trials you have not succumbed to, while learning from but not beating yourself over your failures. Do not be an unrealistic optimist, but do not limit your potential with thoughts of fear and failure. These thoughts should all be discarded. It is important for the health of your self-esteem.

Shun Multitasking

Popular as the idea of multitasking is, it is unnatural and unadvisable. Yes, there are individuals who flourish at handling more than one task at a time, but, for the majority of us, we are at our most productive when we concentrate on completing one activity before moving to another. Multitasking, for many of us, usually originates from impatience. Since we find it almost torturous to settle down and see a task through to completion, we try to bite off more than we can chew. Some examples of this is cooking, listening to a podcast, and sweeping all at the same time or making a call without using handsfree while maneuvering your car on a busy highway. As you can tell from these scenarios, the result may be quite disastrous. Even while online, train your mind to finish a task before opening another app or tab. It may be tempting to quickly check your Instagram feed while doing research, but it is possible to avoid doing that. Simply go to your settings, block certain notifications, and be productively committed to a single activity. When you avoid multitasking, your mind is able to stay attentive for long durations. It would also cause fewer thoughts that clash with each other, ultimately causing less cluttered information in your head.

You Can Relax

It is not wrong for you to chase your dreams and put in the work to bring them to reality. Of course, success does not come easily, and, to this, there is no debate. But the hours of hard work mean that the mind is constantly being pushed to think up solutions and new ideas. If the wheels of the mind are kept in constant motion without due rest, soon it will not be able to function optimally, and this spells disaster for your productivity. It is necessary to find some time for nothing more than relaxation. Go on a trip, visit old friends, kick your feet up and savor the sun warming your face, watch a movie, or spend time with your family. It invigorates the body and helps to free up some space in your mind. If you can, turn off your phones and take a break from social media, business, pop culture news, politics, etc. The mind is the most important asset for human beings and, as such, should be given the most care. Unfortunately, in today's society, mental health is often relegated to the back burner as vices like money, power, and sex are placed at the fore. This should not be. Relax and enjoy your company, and those good people in your life.

Journal It

Maybe you are not one to write down your thoughts and emotions, but, as freeing as this exercise can prove to be, you've got to give it a go. There is so much going on in your head than even you can make sense of. But it is often better understood and tackled when you can get it out of your headspace. And it doesn't have to be the typical notepad that is turned into a diary of emotions and daily experiences. All you need is something to write with and something to write on that is private. You could use your phone for this. The goal of doing this is to allow your mind to operate more smoothly by taking out the noise. What are your worries and concerns? Write down your expectations. This is also good for your memory and can be helpful in pointing you towards the right direction. You can do this as frequently as you feel you must. People who write in journals may observe themselves being significantly less stressed and enjoy a better quality of life. This is because they have dealt with some of their mind clutter and neatly arranged their thoughts. Journals are also a good idea for people with anxiety issues.

You May Need Someone to Talk To

Everybody needs that person or those set of people who they can trust to unburden the weight on their shoulders. This is one reason why people visit psychiatrists, confess to priests, and talk to their pets. We want someone who will listen, not judge or berate us, and help make meaning of the clutter inside our heads. This could be a close friend, family member or, as given in the example above, a shrink or priest. If you feel comfortable, then let the tears fall when talking to that person. After all they should be people you are not ashamed or afraid around. If you are one to keep your emotions caged inside, you may set them free with that person. Also, there is a reason why two heads are said to be better than one. Such people can help you with a different perspective on whatever has had you worried and afraid. You just might find that the challenge was really nothing and, in fact, one to be easily surmounted. Talking it out with someone besides having a back and forth in your head is good for decision making and risk assessment.

Ask These Questions

Is this something you care about? Does someone important to you care about it? Is it important to your happiness? Should your answer be no to all three questions on any issue, then you can safely strike it out of your list of concerns. It is little more than a distraction and should be discarded as you aim towards a decluttered mind. This could also be done after you have written your thoughts in a journal. Review every seemingly pressing concern to see if they pass these questions. As you continue to identify more of these derailing thoughts for what they are, your mind will be clearer. It is necessary that you do this exercise every day or as often as you can. This would prevent your mind from becoming cluttered again either with old issues or new ones. Whether it's a product you want to purchase or a personal project you are about to undertake, ask these questions to determine their worth.

You Must Set Priorities

Without priorities, it would seem like you are on an endless race against the clock and in no particular direction. Everything would bear the same level of importance in your mind and demand your attention equally. When it comes to setting priorities for your life, there is just one rule; the most important things come first. For example, a person without priorities cannot accurately distinguish between the need to live large and have fun, and the importance of saving money. This individual knows that he or she must have their finances in order, but they can't see how buying clothes worth hundreds of dollars and constantly eating out would hurt them. Since this book is about decluttering, consider a person who has to make a choice between tidying up their home and repainting it. There is some similarity between the two choices and, probably, good reasons as to why they need to be done. But if the clutter is affecting joy, concentration, and mental health of the individual, then decluttering must be placed as a priority. If you must spend time thinking and planning, then let it be about those things at the top of your list of priorities.

Mind the Amount of Information You Allow into Your Thoughts

Considering the times we live in, it may seem almost entirely impossible to filter which information gets into our minds. Even as we celebrate the advances in technology and the kind of media we now enjoy, it just might not be all positive. Once upon a time, we could live happily and satisfied without mobile phones. Nowadays, the average person not only owns a smartphone, but depends on it for happiness. To that individual, his or her phone is, often, better company than a real-life person. As a consequence, the information absorbed by the average person in terms of advertisements, news, celebrity gossip, and so on may start to conflict with thoughts that should actually be a priority. Many of us spend more time thinking about this usually irrelevant information than about what could truly be of benefit to us. To declutter your mind, it is necessary that you create a limit as to how much TV you can watch, and time spent on social media or browsing the internet. Go a step further and unsubscribe from websites and magazines that may not be of any true value to you. Decide that whatever information you allow into your conscious and subconscious mind would be relevant and not time wasting, even when it comes to entertainment. By so doing, you afford your mind more space to cater to more pressing issues.

Chapter 9: A Checklist for Your Decluttering

***

Use the guide in Chapter 7 to assist you with this checklist. If you find that your home does not consist of anything in a particular day in this checklist, then take a break on that day and just appreciate all you've done so far.

Week One	
D a y 1	Pick up the trash inside the house and get rid of it.
D a y 2	Gather the little things such as pencils and toothbrushes that have no particular place in your house and arrange them.
D a y 3	Declutter your shelves and other surfaces where you store items.
D a y 4	Search your pockets.
D a y 5	Organize and declutter your refrigerator and food storage spaces.
D a	Organize your books.

y 6	
D a y 7	Arrange the toys in your kids' room(s).

Week Two	
Day 8	Organize your bedroom furniture and decorative items
Day 9	Organize your wardrobe.
Day 10	Tidy up your bedside table and office desk.
Day 11	Declutter your drawers.
Day 12	Check beneath the bed in your bedroom
Day 13	Make some room for those items that have no permanent place in your home.
Day 14	Arrange your accessories, such as wristwatches, sunglasses, bracelets, caps, and so on.

Week Three	
Day 15	Declutter duplicate kitchen utensils.
Day 16	Clean out your wine collection, if you have any.
Day 17	Organize your cleaning equipment.
Day 18	Clean out your pets' toys.
Day 19	Arrange holiday decorations.

| Day 20 | Keep your office supplies in order. |
| Day 21 | Organize your towels and rugs. |

Week Four	
Day 22	Take care of the medications in your house. Expired drugs may be fatal if used.
Day 23	Deal with the DVDs and CDs.
Day 24	Declutter the files on your computer.
Day 25	Clean out your nightstand.
Day 26	Deal with those old photos.
Day 27	Organize your emails today.
Day 28	Organize your regular mail.

Week Five	
Day 29	Get a waste bin for every room and a storage box for the kids' room(s).
Day 30	Tidy up the outside of the house.

Checklist for Routine Decluttering

After this 30-day decluttering exercise, it might have become a habit for you to tidy up and organize your house. Yet there are a few things that would be of immense help in getting you to continue decluttering. The checklist below is for routines which should be done on a daily basis. Use it to ensure you stay committed to cleaning out and organizing your home.

Daily Routine for Decluttering	
1st routine	Have four storage boxes for everyone in the house. Everyone should have their names on their boxes, and they should also be labeled in this manner; donations, trash, repairs, and borrowed. Items that fall into any of those categories should be placed in their respective boxes.
2nd routine	Make your commitment to decluttering public. You may post about it on social media. It is more likely that you will be resolved to continuing with a positive habit when others are aware of it.
3rd routine	Enter each room every morning to see if anything needs to be tidied. If there is, then clean out that room. If you do this daily, it won't be as difficult as the first time to tidy up any particular room.
4th routine	Inform your kids that they will be rewarded for using the labeled storage boxes and keep your promise when they do.

Made in the USA
Columbia, SC
13 October 2023

24435189R00057